From LENIN To The Cross

by

Andrey and Tanya Shpigunov

with

Lars Dunberg

From Lenin to the Cross
by Andrey and Tanya Shpigunov with Lars Dunberg
Published by *Global Action*
7660 Goddard Street, Suite 200
Colorado Springs, CO 80920, U.S.A.

www.globalaction.com
o: 719.528.8728; f: 719.528.8718

ISBN: 978-1-4507-4703-5

Published in the United States by *Global Action*

Cover design: Barten Visual Communications, www.bartenvisual.com
Interior design: Nasko D. Lazarov

Printed in the United States of America
2010 - First *Global Action* Edition

Contents

Introduction

THE ORIGINAL UKRAINE HOPE CENTER WAS BUILT IN 1957 at the eastern tip of Crimea on the outskirts of the city Kerch. At that time the Center served as a pioneer camp for young people and was named as a reminder of the October revolution.

During the period of time of the Soviet Union this facility was utilized for camps that accommodated more than 150 kids at a time. All camp programs were based on and promoted Communist ideology. As a symbol of Communist power and its world dominance, a larger than life memorial statue of Lenin stood in the center of the camp.

From Lenin...
After the fall of the Soviet Union in 1991, neglected and practically in ruins, the camp was abandoned and later placed on the market for auction in early 2002. In early June of 2002, *Global Action* purchased the center. *Global Action*'s primary interest was in the four-story guesthouse adjoining the property. However, with limited resources, *Global Action* knew it would be impossible to outbid other bids, so the decision was made to purchase the camp instead.

To the Cross....
Today on the very spot where the statue of Lenin once stood, a cross stands erect. By the light of a bonfire, and in the very same place where young communists once gathered around the star of the Soviet Union to sing praises to communist ideology, young people now share their stories of Christian faith and conversion and sing praises to Jesus.

Thanks to the hard work of many work teams, the children's buildings were restored to livable conditions. In addition, the entire camp has undergone a massive restoration and modernization of the grounds and facilities. With generous charitable donations for the orphans — abused and neglected children — we have been able to conduct programs year round where children are introduced to Christ and His ministry.

Every summer, camps are held for over 400 children. Each child receives proper meals, love, care and a personal Bible. For some years the Hope Center housed a vocational school for adolescent graduates from orphanages. The goal of this program was to help young people adapt to modern society and receive an education as well as to train them for a profession.

Throughout the school year the Hope Center also holds an after-school program for disadvantaged children. This program provides each child a meal, time and support to complete their schoolwork as well as many other activities that help prevent the kids from falling victim to street life. Lectures are held in high schools to promote a healthy way of life for teenagers. Topics such as the dangers of alcoholism, narcotics, prostitution, and sexually transmitted diseases are presented.

Each year the Hope Center is blessed to receive between four to six trucks filled with humanitarian aid. These supplies are distributed to hospitals and clinics as well as needy, physically challenged and disabled individuals.

Finally, a pastoral training program, Global Module Studies (GLOMOS), has also been held at the Hope Center. This program provides training for current and future ministers.

The Hope Center is a wonderful place! God is working to miraculously change hearts and lives. Not only are the lives of those coming for help transformed, but also the lives of those who work at the Hope Center. We invite you to read on and learn more of the vital ministry of *Global Action*'s Hope Center and how you can be involved.

Lars Dunberg
Colorado Springs
November 2010

Chapter 1

An Empty Promise

Becomes Reality

BARRY FLUTH AND LARS DUNBERG MET FOR THE FIRST time in the Spring of 2001. Long before the Hope Center was even a thought, Barry was ready to go on one of *Global Action*'s more primitive outreach teams and to visit orphans in Crimea.

Barry tells the story:
"In the summer of 2001, a friend and I went on a two-week *Global Action* ministry trip to visit orphans at a camp near the sea in Ukraine. While we were there we joked that maybe I should buy an old resort and turn it into a Christian ministry center. As it turned out this wasn't too far away from what actually happened.

"While at this camp, we helped teach the kids crafts using supplies we had brought with us. We also brought humanitarian aid to distribute at some of the orphanages. Many of the kids were orphans or in the equivalent of a foster care system. We taught Bible lessons for the children each day and were privileged to challenge many kids to follow Christ for the rest of their lives--over half made a commitment to do just that.

"But conditions at these camps were not ideal. Poor sanitation, inadequate ventilation, uncomfortable beds and low-quality food made the camp experience less enjoyable than it could have been for both the Ukrainians and Americans. Also, we were charged high fees for the privilege of using the camp and additional fees seemed to come up after we arrived. We realized that in order to minister effectively year in and year out, a permanent camp would be needed. God seemed to be urging us to explore the possibilities and trust Him for the resources."

In December, Barry Fluth and Rev. Bill Arant from Riverside Alliance Church met with Lars Dunberg from *Global Action* to discuss the possibilities. Lars was not showing much interest. "We are not a bricks and mortar organization," he explained. Further, Lars empasized that *Global Action* is simply not large enough to even dream of investing in buildings.

Barry looked Lars in the eye and stated, "… if we buy a place and give it to you, would you take the responsibility to run it?" Lars, knowing full well that foreigners could not buy property in Ukraine, smiled and committed himself. "Well, if you buy one and give it to us, I will surely run it!" He was certain that this was the last he would ever hear about it.

Barry continues, "…in March of 2002, three other men and I went back to Ukraine, down to the Crimean peninsula to search for a suitable site. We located a facility in the seaport/resort town of Kerch, at the eastern tip of the Crimean peninsula. The town has a population of 200,000 and is strategically located across a narrow straight from Russia, right on the Black Sea. The camp would accommodate 200 people, and the buildings were structurally sound. The Lord worked in a miraculous way. Later that spring, through the gifts of many people who contributed large and small amounts, all the money necessary to buy the camp was raised."

To Lars Dunberg's great surprise, a new camp center was bought at an auction, with his office helping with some of the financial transactions. First the banks stated that all the funds had to be in Ukraine currency — Hrievna. When the sum was deposited in the bank, the message changed. "No, we need it in U.S. dollars." A few days went by with everyone nervously holding their breath. Finally, the bank returned the Hrievna to *Global Action*!

Barry concludes, "In less than a year we went from seeing Ukrainian orphans for the first time to buying a beautiful camp for cash and donating it to a great mission organization. Since then, the task of renovating the facility to bring it up to current codes for camps for orphans has been ongoing. A permanent camp director was installed, and a work team of local Ukrainians was established. Local workers were brought in to handle special tasks. A team of six people from Riverside Church in Monticello went to Ukraine in October 2002 and jump started the water, electrical, plumbing, and heating renovation. Locals worked through the winter. In February 2003 two more teams of twelve volunteers from the U.S. came to the facility to renovate the kitchen, medical building and showers.

"Work continued and three summer camps for children were planned for July of 2003. We finished the work and received our final permit at noon on the day the first camp was to open. Since then at least five camps each summer have ministered to thousands of needy kids.

"The ministry at the Hope Center has mushroomed. Pastoral training, business seminars, humanitarian aid, vocational training, feeding programs and educational programs have all ministered to needy children and adults. The Ukrainian staff has taken ownership of the ministry in a major way. They have sent out teams to other countries to hold camps for children, devised strategies to meet the needs of the street children, and educated those most at risk of prostitution and the sex trade. It has been a thrill and pleasure to see God work through the dedicated Christian workers, a great facility, and His plan for this ministry."

Lars Dunberg contacted his board to update and inform them about the purchase. The board had a policy against bricks and mortar projects. However, they agreed that this was a worthwhile project even though the project could be lost at any time due to the fact that in Ukraine you lease the land and own the buildings, an arrangement uncommon in the West.

Finally all the documentation was complete. A not-for-profit organization, *Global Action* Ukraine, incorporated and the rest is history – thousands of lives impacted for Jesus Christ.

Chapter 2

Passionate Leaders Make the Difference

AS SOON AS THE UKRAINE HOPE CENTER WAS PUR-chased, Lars Dunberg realized that core staff members were needed to operate camps, to help with administration, training of staff and tracking finances. At that point few of the Ukrainian staff were fluent in English. Tom Benz, an employee of *Global Action* and married to a Ukrainian, made several visits to the Hope Center to recruit people. A local pastor, Sergey Frolov—an invaluable help in finding the Center—was asked to help in the development of the Center during this time.

In July, Lars called his friend Jörgen Edelgård in Sweden and asked if he and his wife were interested in giving a few years to Ukraine before they retired. Jörgen and Ingegerd visited the Hope Center, together with Lars and Doreen Dunberg, in August 2002 and decided to return a few weeks later to begin their work.

This is what Jörgen had to say about his visit to the Center:

"When I arrived at the Center the very first time, my immediate thoughts were, 'Fantastic location, enormous potential, but extremely rundown!' Where once there had been toilets, there were only gaping holes.

My wife Ingegerd had run children's camps for International Bible Society in the past, even in Ukraine. I went along with her one year, so I knew roughly what was expected of a decent camp location. I had also seen the needy children, and I knew what a tremendous impact a camp would have in their lives.

Of course, we did not speak any Russian when we came. The language was a great barrier. However, I had some excellent interpreters, and Sergey Frolov worked hard to master his English. Perhaps the biggest challenge was the culture. It was hard for me as a Swede to accept that people did not think for themselves. Generally speaking, the Ukrainians were so accustomed to being told what to do that they did not take individual initiative, and nothing else got done. Instructions had to be as detailed as possible so that no responsibility would rest on the workers. With time, we all learned to understand each other better.

Because of the skills of Sergey Frolov, and despite the corruption ruling the day, we managed to create trust with the authorities. They recognized that *Global Action* and the Hope Center actually could add something useful – like a feather in the hat, so to speak. Through our work together with the authorities, we equipped several hospitals with basic equipment, such as beds, incubators, operating tables and wheelchairs."

For Ingegerd it was hard to understand how children in general were treated, especially the orphans. "It was common to lock children up and harshly punish them, rather than create an atmosphere where the children could enjoy what was happening around them. The Soviet style camp mentality was still deeply rooted in the Crimean soul, even among the first set of staff members. Over a period of time, we finally arrived at the understanding that children were the guests of honor at the camps and were there, not to be suppressed, but to enjoy their time. "

Although Ingegerd suffered with medical problems, she worked relentlessly at the Hope Center. One of the things she loved was to help with the distribution of medical supplies when they finally cleared customs and arrived by truck from Sweden.

Ingegerd tells this story:
"The rumors spread across Kerch in Crimea. At the *Global Action* "Hope Center" there were new crutches, something odd called walkers and even some wheel chairs available for those who needed them.

People with a variety of problems as well as those who were physically challenged turned up at the Hope Center. One of them is Alexander. He is a handsome educated economist approximately 35 years of age. After an accident, he lost his leg. The scars from the accident can still be seen on his face. He could not keep his job as an economist because of his accident. The only solution the government could provide for him was a simple pair of crutches. Beyond that he was on his own.

At the Hope Center, Alexander received new crutches. In his thank you speech he mentioned that his greatest dream was to get an artificial leg, although that would be a financial impossibility for him. Therefore, he was so grateful for the second best—his new crutches!

I was present at the Hope Center that day. I quickly grabbed a measuring tape and helped Alexander measure from the stump of the amputated leg down to the ground. I also took notes of his shoe size on the remaining foot. A few weeks later, when I had returned to Sweden, I called a few people within the health department. I prayed before every phone call until I reached an orthopedist at the orthopedic clinic nearby. He promised to help immediately. 'We have spare parts in the basement, he chuckled, and I'll be happy to help. Come and pick up the artificial leg in a week. As this is for a good cause I will not charge anything for the leg!' It is remarkable what medical professionals keep in their basements!

I picked up the leg, and packed it in a suitcase together with my clothes and some toys for the children at the orphanages in Kerch and took off on my next trip to the Ukraine.

Because of my medical condition—blood clots in my lungs as well as severe asthma—I travel in a wheel chair. I was concerned over what the customs officials would say when the suitcase passed the X-ray machine on arrival in Kiev. No doubt it would identify the extra leg. Since I was in a wheel chair, everyone was polite and did not want to ask any questions.

The next problem was even greater. How would I find Alexander in the city of Kerch? No one had thought of writing down his address or phone number. It did not take many days before I bumped into Alexander on the street. He came limping along on his crutches with one pant leg pinned up with a safety pin. That same night Alexander arrived at the Hope Center to pick up his new leg. I suggested to him that he practice using it at home first. So, Alexander took his leg with him in the suitcase and hobbled home.

A week later he returned to the Hope Center proudly showing his new pair of shoes on both legs and reporting that the artificial leg fitted perfectly. Alexander was so pleased that his tears began to flow when he thanked the people at the Hope Center, thanked God, the Swedish people and its government!"

"The greatest joy right now," concludes Jörgen, "is the fact that we are not needed any more and have not been for some time. Very competent staff members have taken over, and today the Hope Center functions in a way we would barely have thought possible eight years ago."

Two staff members — a young married couple--were there almost from the very beginning. Tanya and Andrey Shpigunov.

Andrey tells his story:

"I was born in the city of Kerch, Crimea, Ukraine, which at that time was part of the USSR. My father worked as a builder. My mother had many jobs including cook, mailperson, and train attendant. Most of my childhood was spent in Kerch. We lived in a shared living space called the barracks. Four members of my family shared one room while the kitchen and bathroom were shared with about five other families. In 1979, we received a small one-room apartment from the government. It was not much, but it was better than the previous living space.

My father often drank far too much so my mother had to take us away to live with my grandmother for periods of time. My parents divorced and for a while lived separately; eventually they moved back together but remained divorced. In 1983 I was blessed with a new brother, and the five of us lived in a small 170 square foot apartment. Mother was in line to receive a larger apartment, but the government never provided one.

Just before I turned fifteen I became involved with bad company and started smoking, drinking and taking drugs. After finishing eighth grade I studied to become a professional welder. I was a good student, but the friends around me turned out to be a bad influence. I continued to get deeper into drugs and alcohol.

While still studying in 1991, one of my friends told me that there is a Christ and that there are Christian people. He invited me to a Christian service that often was held in an apartment. There I found out more about Christ and the Holy Spirit. Just as my friend had told me, the Holy Spirit gets you higher than drugs. I repented right there and then. I had joy, a desire to go to the Christian services, and a fire in my heart. But after two weeks of going to the services, a group of us fell back into using heavy drugs. These friends were worse than the ones I had before, and suddenly I found myself deeper into drugs. All of this required more money and led me to steal as well as to forcing people to give me money. Lying, stealing, alcohol and drugs began to rule my life. All the money that came in was spent on my addictions.

I remember one instance when two partners and I robbed a store. We cut the wire of the alarm system and backed out to hide and see if the cops would come. The police never came. We broke into the store via the window and grabbed as many goods as we could carry in our bags. We escaped with huge amounts of money in goods, but all of it was spent on drugs. Every Sunday we would drive to market to sell the goods we had stolen.

One by one my friends began to disappear. Some were killed, some shot to death, others were maimed, some put in jail, and others simply overdosed. When I was twenty I, along with two other guys, were out of drugs. Both of them were experiencing strong withdrawals so they started to pop pills. I joined in with them. For about four days we popped pills. On the fifth day a friend brought the heavy drugs. I fell asleep while two of my friends went to prepare the injections. When I woke up they were gone. I waited for them to return but they didn't come back. I decided to take the drugs by myself. Next thing I know, I am in the hospital. I had overdosed.

As soon as I was released from the hospital I went back to try to find them, but both of them had died from an overdose. They were both younger than me. One was nineteen and the other one was eighteen. I was very lucky to be alive. Back in those days it was extremely hard to call for an ambulance. If you did, it usually took at least half an hour before the ambulance arrived. However, in my case they turned up just in time. My lungs stopped functioning when I arrived at the hospital, but the doctors were able to revive me.

During my six years of this intense lifestyle, over twenty of my friends died — either killed or overdosed — most of them were below twenty-five. In 1996 a friend and I became heavily intoxicated and decided to steal a car. After a few kilometers we hit an electric pole just as a police cruiser stopped close by. We exited the car and ran for our lives as the police chased after us, shooting at us. Somehow we managed to escape. The stolen vehicle turned out to be not just any regular car but it belonged to someone with strong ties with the criminal underworld. They soon found us and demanded money - $4,000!

After that incident, I began thinking deeply about what kind of life I was living. The criminals were looking for me. The government was looking for me. I did not have any documents that would enable me to leave the country or even go to work. My situation seemed to have no escape. I began to get drunk on a regular basis over the next few months.

Then one day I met one of my old friends who I knew went to church. He was now a minister in that church. He did not try to preach to me or say anything about Christ. He just listened. I was amazed by his peaceful countenance and the joy in his eyes. I wanted to visit the church where he ministered so I asked him when and where I could attend a church service. Once I attended this church I wanted more and more and came back every week.

In March of 1997 I was invited to a birthday party for someone in the church, and it was there I accepted Christ. As soon as I asked Christ into my life, something changed within me. I felt lighter. I knew that I no longer had an addiction to drugs or alcohol. I was free. I knew that all those old things were not a part of me anymore. God had set me free! Later I was able to obtain a passport. No one was searching for me any longer. In September that year, God blessed me with a job.

Tanya and I went to church together, but we became closely acquainted while we were in Bible school. I began to understand that she was the one woman for me. In 2001 we were married.

I worked at the Hope Center—first as a guard—but after a while I went to Moscow to help my father. In 2004 when the work with my father was over I had a desire to be a part of the International Vocational Academy program at the Hope Center. I had to make a choice: either continue to work in Moscow with good pay or return and work at the Hope Center as a security guard with little pay. I went back to serve the children at the Hope Center. In the summer of 2006 Tanya and I were invited to be the directors of the Hope Center. I have never regretted working for *Global Action*. Our family is blessed to work here. I have important work and the most wonderful family. God has blessed us with a place to live, a car to drive, and most of all we have the satisfaction of doing God's will.

Since God began His work in my life I have had a passion for ministry to teens and young adults. Following this calling in my life, I'm blessed to serve at the Hope Center working with the youth in the vocational school as well as the many other ministries. I do know that during times of hardship it is very important to have someone near you to guide you in the way of the truth. God has given me the opportunity and blessing to serve here, and I am so thankful to Him for it."

Tanya's story:
"I was born in Russia in the city of Kaluga not far from Moscow. I grew up in a typical communist family of working class parents. My father worked as an electrician, and mother as an accountant. I heard the Gospel for the first time when I was eleven. My uncle, who lived in Kerch, Crimea, was a believer and he encouraged us to attend some evangelistic meetings in Moscow, so my mother and I went. I accepted Christ there but my mother did not. Our city did not have any evangelical churches so when we went to Kerch during the summer holidays, I would always go to church there. I never missed a service or church event. I had such a strong thirst for God.

When I was twelve my parents divorced, and my mother took me and my brother and moved down to Ukraine. I did not take the divorce of my parents lightly. There were moments when I simply did not want to live. In those moments Jesus became my closest friend. After the move, our family encountered much hardship. We did not have a place to live and my mother had to work many hours. I remember a time when having a full loaf of bread was a rare and joyful event.

I always wanted to work with children. When I turned twelve I had the opportunity to work with children in Sunday school. After completing high-school I went on to a university and prepared to be a teacher. Throughout my time at the university I did not have money to pay for my studies. However, God always provided for me in miraculous ways. Since the age of fifteen I had to work while still studying, first as a nanny and later, while at the university, as a counselor in a kindergarten. During all this time I continued to be active in church and work with children.

Andrey and I met at church. We became good friends, talked a lot and at times went out together. That is when I began to find out about Andrey's criminal past. Sometimes while out on a walk together he would point out places where his friends had been killed or the places he used to rob. It was not as romantic as a walk on the beach!

The very first time he proposed to me I said, "No! You're old, fat, and bald." But Andrey continued to show signs of affection. One time, when I went to the university in Simferopol for a month, Andrey would call me every evening at ten. We talked anywhere from thirty minutes to over an hour. Every time he called I asked him to stop calling me. I told him, "You distract me from my studies, so please don't call me anymore." But he continued to call, and I would continue to talk to him for hours, while still asking him to stop.

Then one day, it became 10:00 p.m. and Andrey did not call. A few minutes later I looked at the clock and it showed 10:05 p.m., but the phone was still silent; 10:20 p.m. and still nothing. At 10:30 p.m. I began to worry. "Why is he not calling me?" That is when I realized that I was actually waiting for his call and that Andrey meant more to me than just a friend.

That evening Andrey did call at around 11:00 p.m. That is when I agreed to meet him and we began to have more serious talks about getting married. He no longer seemed fat, old and bald to me. Finally, in 2001 we were married. A year later our first son, Alesha, was born. *Global Action* bought the Hope Center and our pastor, Sergei Frolov, invited us to work there.

I began my work at the Hope Center as a counselor, and I remember thinking, "This is what I want to dedicate my life to." Here I met hundreds of children who were in similar or even worst circumstances than I. In the past God had always used people who supported me and helped me. At the Hope Center I realized that I could help and influence others.

I saw that happening in the life of a girl that came to the Hope Center from an orphanage. As I got to know her better I found out that her story was very similar to mine. Her parents often drank, she was left hungry and ate only two or three times a week. Her food usually consisted of nothing but bread. She was an adolescent, about to be released from the orphanage. She told me, 'You are lucky. You have a job. You have food, family and a place to live but I have none of those things.' Then she asked me, 'Where will I find a job when I get out of the orphanage? I have no education. Who wants to hire an orphan with no experience?'

This young girl told me that she was jealous of me. At that point I had such a strong desire to grab her, shake her, and say, 'Just believe! We have a very big God! It is because of Him that

I have a job, family and education. He has the power to do the same for you! Just stay faithful to Him.' We continue to talk via phone.

One of the greatest gifts of this center is an opportunity to serve others – like this girl – to let them know that they are not alone and that there is hope! That is what I like most about this place – the opportunity it provides to serve and change lives, to put an imprint on someone, to share God's gift, to share God's love with children who don't know what it means to be loved.

In 2010 we had our second child, a boy we named Iliya. Now we are twice as happy with two boys. This year Alesha is eight, and he dreams of becoming a translator at the Hope Center. As for my parents, my mother is still alive, but she is not a believer. However, there have been many moments when she has seen miraculous things in my life as a testimony to God. I pray and believe that a moment will come when she will accept the Lord as her Savior. I only see my father – who is not a believer – once every two years.

God's work here is just beginning. I believe that many thousands of lives will be changed. There are so many needs and possibilities to help here at the Hope Center. I believe that God has laid a foundation. It is my prayer that we will be able to continue to build upon it and complete His work to touch many more lives in the years to come."

There was quite a vacuum after the Edelgårds retired and returned to Sweden. *Global Action* filled it by inviting people from the USA to serve as interns for longer periods of time. Jim and Sherrie Hunt from Texas served us. Sherrie worked helping us with our English, and Jim is a superb maintenance man as well as a good instructor at the International Vocational Academy.

Sarah and Matt Gaw gave us almost two years of service. Matt was already on staff with *Global Action*. He came on a short-term trip to the Hope Center and lost his heart here. Returning home he convinced not only *Global Action* but also his wife – who had never been to Ukraine--that this was their future. On a cold, wintry day the whole family, with young son Campbell, arrived at the Hope Center. What an invaluable help they have been!

Here are Matt's reflections:

"My first experience with the Hope Center was an intensely emotional one. That experience was what I needed for the Lord to get my attention. All my previous mission trip experiences – and indeed all visits outside of my country – had been in Latin America. I felt that when the time came to move abroad it would be to the Spanish-speaking world. Fortunately for us, I left my heart in Ukraine that summer, and the timing was perfect for us to return as a family.

"Unfortunately, we did not arrive to the balmy Mediterranean weather I had enjoyed the previous summer. We arrived in the harsh, cold winter of the Eurasian steppe. Initially we were engaged in acclimatization. I was thrown into the important task of driving. Little did I know what a valuable commodity my drivers license would be. On the second day after we arrived, I joined a ministry team to participate in a feeding program in the Village of Mayak. On the way home I was informed that I was to take over the driving responsibilities for this vital ministry, even though I had only seen the route once and never sat behind the wheel of a car outside the US.

"We entered the ministry of the Hope Center as very different people from those who preceded us. Jim Hunt and I are of different generations. Further, we have come from different educational, professional and experiential backgrounds. This was also true for Sheri and Sarah. Thankfully, Andrey and Tanya understood and embraced this fact. We were given access to all levels of operation so that we could know in what area the Lord was calling us to work.

"While most of the Hope Center's ministries take place outside of the busy summer camp period, we found some of our most fulfilling moments during those months. We discovered the inherent advantage to our ability as insiders to understand the necessary elements of the operation of the camp and then convey that to the visiting English-speaking teams. What might have become a time-consuming or complicated misunderstanding could often be avoided by our mediation. It wasn't something for which we had any particular talent, but rather the nature of being able to see both perspectives.

"Under Andrey and Tanya's tutelage our tasks, level of involvement and contributions evolved based on our gifts, talents and passions. They respected our position as a bridge between the U.S. and Ukrainian branches of *Global Action*.

"Were it not for the need to return to the U.S. for the birth of our second child, I'm sure we would still be in Ukraine at the Hope Center with our friends. Over our two years of service, we developed such a close working and personal relationship with this extraordinary couple that I can honestly say that they will be lifelong friends."

Other interns have served for long periods of time and have been an enormous help. People such as Naomi Hyttsten and Judith Chan, just to mention a few. They have been spiritual leaders and an example for all of us. Seeing their selfless work in the Hope Center made us realize what it means to work for the glory of the Lord.

Chapter 3

The Camps

THE PRIMARY MOTIVATION FOR PURCHASING THE Hope Center was to conduct summer camps for the orphans as *Global Action* had done for several years previously. To accomplish this in previous years, *Global Action* rented facilities in various locations.

The Hope Center camp needed massive renovation. Toilets and hand basins arrived from Sweden, as well as beds, mattresses and bed linen. Some material was purchased. Work teams came to make the camp ready for the very first camps in 2003. We learned many lessons that first summer.

By the summer of 2004, we had a full five-camp summer but not without glitches. There was tension between the Ukrainian staff and the visiting teams. Some of the Ukrainians thought it would be better if the Westerners did not come at all but just sent the money. Some wanted the camps run in a traditional Soviet-style camp. This horrified many of the Westerners.

During the first camp in 2004 several of the Western leaders gathered together and made a call to the president of *Global Action*, Lars Dunberg. It was their suggestion that the camp be closed down immediately. They stated that the camp would be a waste of money if no changes were made. It was a time of soul searching and loving confrontation. In spite of our difficulties, children came to know Jesus Christ, and experienced love and care from both the Ukrainian and Western team members.

By the end of summer 2005, it became clear that Jörgen and Ingegerd Edelgård could not stay much longer and that permanent Ukrainian leadership needed to be in place to make the Hope Center function well. Andrey had left the Hope Center for a while and was working in Moscow when *Global Action* extended an invitation to Tanya and me to come and take over the leadership of the camp. What a joy and privilege!

Since then, working together with the staff locally, the visiting teams and with *Global Action* leadership has been a joy. As with any ministry organization, this joy is combined with challenges, financial pressures and an enormous trust in God's provision. Add to this the fact that literally thousands of children have found a new meaning in their lives and many have found the Savior as their best friend.

The Hope Center camps take up all summer. Group after group come to spend their ten days in paradise. Kids meet the living God. Time flies by. One day kids are excitedly waiting for the opening ceremony to begin and before we know it the ten days are behind us.

What was camp like? What impressions did camp make on the kids and adults? What did the participants of those marvelous events experience during their ten days at the most wonderful place on earth - the Hope Center? One thing we know for sure — every life was changed for the better.

For the past eight years the Hope Center has welcomed disadvantaged kids and orphans. Christian summer camps are one of the most important events of the Hope Center's year. Throughout the entire year the personnel gets the Center ready to welcome kids from orphanages of various regions in Ukraine. The creation of a unique atmosphere of kindness, love, concern and care depends on our personnel's devotion to the Lord. Sharing the Gospel is the reason people of different ages and backgrounds travel to the Hope Center. They care neither about time and money nor the hardships they face following the calling of Christ to "*go and make disciples of all nations*" (Matt. 28:19 NIV).

The International Teams

Teams come from all over but most teams come from the U.S. A mix of teenagers, grandmothers and children together with their parents — each full of anxiety and enthusiasm — looking forward to introducing kids to the living God. Other teams come from Sweden and the U.K. ready to share God's love through long arms and caring hearts.

Every summer a group of interns stays through several camps and acts as summer staff. Many of them return at their own expense to serve year after year. Without them the summers would more difficult.

The Ukrainian Team Staff

The Hope Center staff does everything possible to assist the teams. Daily, the cooks and kitchen workers surprise everyone with their culinary skills. When President Lars Dunberg comes to visit, the cooks are sure to serve him his favorite – a plate of cheese! The cleaning staff members make sure the grounds and buildings are well maintained. Medical staff skillfully and tenderly takes care of each child and adult. Counselors spend twenty-four hours a day with the kids to help them adapt to the new environment at the camp. The Hope Center directors are always in touch and coordinate the work of the all staff.

Volunteers

People who sincerely love kids help voluntarily wherever they are needed. They clean buildings, assist counselors and support cooks. They do whatever is necessary with fervor and diligence!

Interpreters

"Demolishing the misunderstandings between languages makes God's truth available." This is the motto of the camp interpreting team. They work diligently and tirelessly as one cohesive unit to overcome any language barrier.

A Typical Camp

When the children arrive, the International Team welcomes them warmly. Decorated with balloons everywhere, the Center turns into an inviting place for children. Interestingly, some of the young American volunteer workers do not differ very much from the kids by age and easily establish friendly relationships with each other. The campers come into a new world full of joy, care and love created by kids from another continent.

Camp life quickly starts with early morning exercises. It was not a secret that the kids were not happy about morning workouts. This soon changed as everyone enjoyed learning the dance routines. Before we knew it everyone began looking forward to practicing the routines each morning.

Well-organized activities—as well as bedtime stories— make the time interesting and unforgettable for each child. Members of the international team organize cheerful morning activities for the kids. The girls dance and the boys work on strength and stamina.

Daily Bible lessons are a thought-provoking event for each child. Both adults and kids take an active part in the Bible lessons. Each session begins with the singing of joyful songs. They not only sing and dance; they listen to songs about God, prayer, kindness and love. Each child receives a new Bible to bring with them to every lesson. It is now an important gift for the children and a lesson book for the week. Through the week kids take their first steps toward a better understanding of God.

Bible lessons capture the attention of the children. One year the plot of the story had an Indiana Jones theme with Sevastopol Jones on a quest to find the greatest treasure of all. During his dangerous adventure, Sevastopol Jones revealed Bible stories that led the kids to Jesus — the greatest treasure. The action got the kids involved and challenged them to reconsider their life values.

Craft time is a special activity at every camp. Since Ukrainian kids consider crafts an activity for little kids, at the Hope Center kids began to see the process of crafting in a new way. It becomes an exciting time for them when they are able to make something with their hands. They discover their artistic potential. The "box kite" was a great project that touched boys' hearts and got the girls involved as well. The kids were very interested in making masks of animals, bracelets, and puzzle pictures. They also make picture frames into which they put pictures of their friends from their wards. Some of the crafts include: origami, painting, drawing and making masks and bracelets which are much loved by kids and adults. Everyone can make their own unique item and demonstrate their talent. The music station is the most popular among the interest stations. At this station children can learn to play the recorder and dance to the tunes of a skilled guitar player.

All ten days of camp are action-packed! The whole camp almost explodes with shouts as everyone gathers for the volleyball competition. Fans make signs to cheer on their favorite teams. The players never let you down. They play very hard to show their gratitude to their fans.

The game of "biffer" is another favorite the children enjoy. The new rules make the game more dynamic. Children wait impatiently for the talent show so they can demonstrate their skills. Due to their passion and originality, dances, songs, skits and recitation are big hits with the audience.

Children are always deeply moved by the skit about the sacrifice of Jesus that demonstrates God's love for us. Tears on the children's faces testify that the process of spiritual birth has begun. During bedtime stories, the children share their impressions and many give their hearts to God, accepting Jesus as their personal Savior. It is a true victory!

A powerful movement of the Holy Spirit took place one year during the salvation skit. Kids from different houses joined together and prepared performances of worship to the Lord. The performances included singing, reading poems, and skits about God's love. Jesus was the message of every performance.

The skit performed by the International Team—a mime of the song "Everything" by Lifehouse—pulled on the hearts of everyone in the camp. The skit showed the yearning that God has to be in a relationship with us. It reminded us that we get so distracted with other things such as boyfriends, girlfriends, money, alcohol, and other self-destructive behaviors in an effort to find our worth. Many of the campers could identify with the message of this skit. It ended with a dramatic representation of how God's mercy and love allows us to be free from such strongholds. No one could keep from crying and no one wanted to leave. The kids made themselves comfortable around the stage while international team members worshipped in song. Forgetting the language barrier, the kids tried to sing along. The songs touched their hearts and caused them to understand God's love. The Holy Spirit came and ministered in a mighty way. It was as if Jesus was in their presence telling them, "I am with you. I am the living and loving God."

When the time comes to say good-bye, it is hard to do so. All the kids cry as if they are losing their family. These ten days changed their hearts forever. Now they can anticipate Christ who will live in their new hearts and be with them always.

The Lord calls us to spread His Gospel all around the world. He calls people of different ages to reveal God's truth and to demolish chains of Satan. Come, stand in line with those who are ready to respond to the call of our Lord Jesus Christ! "*Do not merely listen to the word, and so deceive yourselves. Do what it says*" (James 1:22 NIV).

The kids - Who Are They?

The kids come from a variety of places: state run orphanages; orphan centers across the Ukraine; disadvantaged homes in Crimea where children live under difficult circumstances; from individuals who care for orphans and need the additional support of a camp atmosphere. As we interact with these kids we realize that they do not come to us by accident. God saw each of their lives and brought them to a Christian camp so that they would have the opportunity to meet Him personally.

Here are a few of the stories of children whose lives have been touched through the ministry of the Hope Center.

Sasha is an orphan from the Ukraine who attended some of our very first camps. In a letter to us he wrote: "Thank you for letting me come to the Hope Center. It is my paradise! I live on the streets in Evpatoria, and I am 14 years old. One of my buddies told me he had been invited to a Christian camp and would I come along? I thought, Boring…but I was so hungry and decided, I'll be there for a few days and eat well and then take off. I have been able to stay through two camps. Everyone is so kind! I have been respected although I am a wild one! I have learned about Jesus and found out what He thinks about me. Last Thursday, in the morning session, I asked Jesus to come into my life. Now I am another person. I am not leaving here alone. The Lord is with me, and I will continue to read the Bible you gave me every morning. The Hope Center must be Paradise. Please promise me that I can return next summer!"

Fedya came from a rehab center in Kiev. When he first came to the camp he continually worried that he would not be able to return to the rehab center. He would ask if someone would be picking him up. He always seemed anxious. We learned that this stemmed from an earlier experience. His mother never returned to pick him up from summer camp. He was then sent to a rehab center. Fedya was devastated that his own mother would abandon him. His counselor informed us that Fedya's mother had been using alcohol during her pregnancy. As a result he now suffers from mental delay.

His mother was once a famous Olympian during the era of the Soviet Union. After the collapse of the Soviet Union she no longer had any support, she lost her status and hid her disappointments in a high level of alcohol intake. Fedya always seemed anxious and afraid that if he acted up he would be given injections to make him behave better. It wasn't until he participated in crafts that we noticed a release of this anxiety. It was the one time that you could actually see his body relax and have some freedom from his fears. It's amazing to see how God can use such a task to minister to a person's innermost being.

Pavlina comes from a large family with four sisters. Both her parents struggled with alcoholism. Her mother died in a fire and soon after her father left the family. It was a traumatic time for the girls. Abandoned by both parents, they were left alone to care for themselves. They were sent to a rehab center in Kiev, where they all reside to this day. Pavlina had the privilege of coming to our camp as a holiday. Unfortunately, because of her tragic life story she had a hard time enjoying herself. She had great difficulty interacting with people and did not want to participate in any activities. As the week continued on, we saw how God worked in her and helped her to open up to others around her. Joy entered her life and she started to make friends and lasting memories. By the end of the camp, she was crying when she had to say goodbye to new friends. She had become attached to the camp and people who showed her hope.

Nikolai or Kola, as he is also called, was housed with our oldest children. Kola was considered a hyperactive child. He always seemed to be getting into trouble. He continually came into conflict with other campers and counselors. He had little respect for the Bible lessons and often laughed during prayer time. Instead of taking offense to this or responding in anger, the counselors and team members got down on their knees and prayed diligently for him. Two days later, Kola asked for prayer. The bedtime stories were presented in his room and an immediate change was noticed.

In the past his mother did not make enough income to support her children. She struggled to teach Nikolai how to control himself. Her frustration often turned into beatings which in turn made Kola angrier inside.

Kola, who was in desperate need of a father figure, was introduced to God as his heavenly Father. It is our continued prayer that Kola will seek the guidance of the heavenly Father. When he left, he said he wanted to become more obedient and to pray more. The Bible tells us *"Ask and it will be given to you"* (Matt. 7:7).

Nazar lives in an orphan center in Alexandria. An orphan center is a government institution for children. The rights of their parents have been taken away. Nazar has lived in this center for the past seven years as a refuge from his mother. He told us some of his story, but only Nazar can truly know all the pain and heartache he has gone through.

Nazar's mother is a violent alcoholic. She often took out her anger on Nazar. On one occasion she tried throwing him over the 4th floor balcony. Miraculously Nazar's life was spared. She tried selling him so she could buy more vodka. The betrayal from his own mother deeply wounded Nazar's soul. Although this occurred more than seven years ago, it continued to haunt him. While Nazar was at the Hope Center, he made a very difficult but important decision—he wanted to forgive his mom like God had already done for him. This was an important victory in his life.

Zamir, Firishta, Minoza, Kanishek-- four siblings—came to camp as part of an Afghani family who had fled to Ukraine to escape the war. Ukraine has become their home but their parents, having no ties in the country, have struggled to support their children. They finally were forced to send their children to the orphan center in Alexandria. It was the only way for the children to get the food and the education they needed.

Coming to summer camp and visiting Crimea has been an unexpected treat for these kids. Each of them showed enthusiasm to learn about God and wholeheartedly participated in all activities. When they returned to camp the following year it was with sadness in their hearts. Just a few days' earlier, drug addicts looking for money had murdered their father. But the children enjoyed their time at camp where they had an opportunity to hear about the hope they have in Christ.

For about two years Anton had been living with his brother down in the sewage wells. There he came in contact with the practice of inhaling glue and gas. A charitable organization working with street kids intervened and saved him from starvation. To provide some light in the dark wells, the boys would dip a wire in gas and light it on fire. Once when Anton was preparing such a lamp, he accidently spilled some gas on himself. Flaming gas engulfed him immediately and his back was seriously burned. Shortly after that accident, he was admitted into an orphanage where he found out that his mother had died of a drug overdose at the age of 27.

Nickolay's parents were alcoholics. His parents told him that they were leaving but would be back very soon. They locked the house and left. For 48 hours six-year-old Nickolay and his elderly grandparents were locked inside. Finally, the neighbors had to break the door to set them free. Nickolay has not seen his parents since. His invalid grandfather, who participated in the Afghan war and the Chernobyl disaster, began drinking and soon died. The grandmother brought Nickolay to the orphanage.

Ira was raised by her alcoholic mother who did not work. Her father was recently released from jail. He never returned to the family. Ira does all the housework. She is taking a class in voice and raises money for it by selling empty bottles. Ira has a wonderful singing voice. She brings us joy each time she sings.

Vika's and Violetta's mother died of a drug overdose. Their aunt became their guardian. Vika has limited physical abilities due to length of limb discrepancies.

Zahar learned to survive at an early age. His Ukrainian mother was a prostitute and abandoned him in a Gypsy village when he was nine months old. His Gypsy father was sent to jail for dealing and trafficking in drugs. His mother eventually returned to reclaim him but continued her life as a prostitute. She would tie infant Zahar to the leg of the bed and feed him from a pot like a dog. Zahar was taken away from his mother and placed in a mental hospital to be re-socialized to act like a human being. Then Zahar was sent to live with his grandmother and aunt. He became accustomed to getting lots of attention and having his own way. He learned to treat others as he was once treated: with a short-temper, anger, and violence. In the summer of 2009, seven-year-old Zahar came to the *Global Action* Hope Center Camp. When he arrived he continued to act out of anger. The staff responded to him in love, patience and kindness. As the camp progressed, Zahar began to treat others with the same love shown to him. He met other children without families and gained a new appreciation for his own family. His grandmother was volunteering in the camp and saw firsthand the changes that took place in Zahar. In the ten days of camp, God's love began to replace his anger and bitterness.

The majority of the kids coming to the Hope Center from Russia come from families destroyed by alcoholism. When Diana was only a little girl she lost her father. Her mother resorted to drinking, eventually losing her home and becoming a vagrant. When her mother was deprived of her parental rights, Diana was taken to a specialized school. Her mother wrote Diana letters infrequently. Recently she arrived at the school to visit after an absence of three years. Diane was shocked at what she saw. Her mother was dirty, she had lost her teeth and was wearing rags. The child was deeply impacted. She worries about her mother very much.

Diana often has nervous breakdowns that lead to her cutting herself. She has many scars on her right arm as evidence of her emotional instability. At the beginning of the camp Diana would lock herself inside a shell during nightly discussions. She kept silent and paid no attention to us. After a few days, instead of silence, she would come up to tell us good night with a pleasing attitude. It was the beginning of her transformation. At the end of the week we asked who had invited Jesus into their hearts. At that moment Diana raised her hand with the other girls. It was right after the salvation skit. It was a victory for love over disappointment and emptiness.

Roza is a sociable and cheerful Gypsy girl. Her mother is in prison for dealing drugs. Roza's sister moved to Kiev where she is engaged in prostitution. Roza lives with her uncle and does all the housework just to try to please him. She has now moved to a rehabilitation center to be with people who understand her and can help her. When she came to camp her eyes beamed with joy and happiness. With her adult responsibilities far away her childhood returned, leaving grief and sorrow behind her. Roza loves singing during Bible lessons. Her natural artistry and musical talent compelled her to get involved. As she left camp, Roza cried silently. In her eyes we could see the sadness that her time at camp was over so quickly.

Ruslan is 11 years old. He has been diagnosed with cerebral spastic infantile paralysis as a result of birth trauma but this does not stop the boy's joyful attitude. From the very beginning of the camp Ruslan shone like a little sun. He was so happy to find new friends, be by the sea and to have people who protected and took care of him. Ruslan enjoyed outdoor games. He spent a lot of time on the basketball court playing with his new friends. At home his mother has been drinking heavily for the past few years and his father is being treated in the tuberculosis rehabilitation center. He has many problems he does not want to think about.

Ruslan impatiently waited for the bedtime stories. This was the time when he could ask the questions that developed while reading his new Bible. Ruslan is sure that God can and will cure him and enable him to achieve great things.

Kristina lives at the children`s rehabilitation center for orphans and street children in Kiev. Currently, 25 children live there permanently. Fifteen of those children were brought to the Hope Center for a summer break. Many of the kids have lived on the streets for years. It is very difficult for them to forget about the law of the street so quickly.

Kristina is a recent addition to the center. She arrived with serious psychological trauma. At the age of six, she suffered from physical and sexual abuse at the hands of the men in her mother's life. Her mother, a chronic alcoholic, did not care about her three daughters. The children were suffering from hunger and abuse.

Around other children, Kristina always tried to get the adults' attention. She often yelled, acted out and beat the other children. This was followed by remorse and desperate cries of, "No one loves me and no one wants to be my friend." Very often, she spent time in her room playing with her invisible friend and talking to herself. Adults saw what was happening with this child and they prayed for her every day. They played and talked to her, tried to help her understand that she is special and that she has a friend, Jesus, who is always there for her and who loves her very much. We were interested to note that Kristina always asked to eat. Even during bedtime stories, when members of the International Team came, she would ask if they had food.

As time went by, Kristina became completely different. She regulated her behavior with other children and met her new friend Luda, with whom she played everyday. By the end of the camp she had stopped taking bread from the canteen and asking the adults for food. The salvation skit and message about Jesus surfaced a lot of questions. The slow process of spiritual healing had begun.

Maxim's story is a tragic one. At the young age of 12 Maxim and his older brother and sister lost both parents in one day. His father suffered heart problems while driving and caused the accident that killed them both. His brother brought Maxim to the Hope Center in a terrible emotional condition. The boy was hiding behind buildings and crying. Members of the International and Ukrainian Teams, full of God's love and compassion, didn't abandon him but gave him all the attention possible. Soon Maxim started participating in singing during the Bible lessons. Now he enjoys singing and has a good voice. At the closing ceremony Maxim, together with the International Team, sang his favorite song. Everyone fell in love with him. Maxim still comes to the Hope Center to visit his new friends as God helps him to overcome his grief and loss.

Isolda is just one tragedy of a tortured childhood. Looking into her eyes as she arrives at the camp you can see that her life has not been easy.

Her unusual name - Isolda - stressed her inborn beauty. Outwardly, she did not differ much from others within her peer group. She was not very talkative and reacted harshly to any attention from the boys. After a while we established a friendship with her. It was obvious that she was ready to connect. Isolda would ask for advice, she shared her personal "girl" concerns with us or would just quietly sit with us. Then one evening Isolda shared her family story with us.

Isolda was born in Volgograd, Russia. Her mother had just turned 19 when Isolda was born. She was not married. The young woman had to raise the child by herself, receiving no help from her family. When Isolda was one-year old her mother went to work in a shoe shop. Her mother would leave her with neighbors. This situation did not last long. Isolda's mother started drinking with new acquaintances she met at the shoe shop. Soon she abandoned her job and the tough life began. Isolda's mother saw the source of all her problems in the pretty little girl so she started taking out her anger on Isolda. She would not give her food for several days. The cruelty kept escalating. Isolda was beaten often. Her mother drank alcohol constantly. Isolda had to walk around the neighborhood to ask for food. Neighbors would call the police but they did not deprive the mother of her parental rights. The situation went from bad to worse when Isolda's mother began using drugs. Isolda would often find herself in places where people were using drugs.

Isolda did not attend kindergarten and did not interact with other children. Instead, drug addicts surrounded her. Her mother would make her get money for buying drugs, alcohol and cigarettes. Isolda would pick up glass bottles and sell them or she begged . She did everything possible to prevent her mother from punishing her. Isolda also confided that on numerous occasions she watched her mother being raped. Poor Isolda was exposed to and experienced unspeakable horrors.

Once she and her mother were almost buried alive - only a miracle saved them! Shortly after this incident, relatives took Isolda to a town in Ukraine. Unfortunately, she spent only a short time there. By the time Isolda was ten years old she was placed in an orphanage where they taught her to read and write. It was there that she found out that her mother had been jailed for murdering her boyfriend. Isolda was aware that it could have been her instead because her mother tried to murder her several times. "I always dreamt that my mother would call me 'honey' and that she would be my best friend forever", Isolda told us with tears in her eyes.

As we spent time with Isolda we realized that she wanted forgiveness, love and Jesus. God said, "Even if your mother abandons you and everybody abandons you, I shall not abandon you." Bible lessons, bedtime stories, and interaction with Christians began the process of change in this young girl. She responded by hearing the Word of God and observing people's caring attitude and concern for her. For the first time in her life Isolda was reflecting upon the fact that she truly wanted forgiveness. The deep, painful, bleeding wounds in her heart will not be healed right away. The process is ongoing.

Among the boys from the internat (the boarding school cum orphan school) was a thirteen-year-old named Egor who had recently accepted Jesus. We were excited about how he was spreading the Gospel among his new friends. While playing ping pong or basketball, he told them about Christ and got them engaged and interested through his reflections upon life and its purpose. Even after the games would stop, they kept talking about the Father who will never betray or abandon them. We were amazed and thrilled to see God working 24-hours a day in a powerful way.

Artyom and Jenya Samoylov are eight- and nine-years-old. During the summers their great-grandmother — almost 80 years old — leaves them at the orphanage so she can plant her garden and have food for the children in the winter. The boys' parents are in prison and deprived of their parental rights. Their great-grandmother is their guardian. The boys were brutally beaten by their father. Through this painful experience their father taught Artyom and Jenya a very important lesson - only the strong survive. When they arrived at camp they immediately started exercising their power and asserting their superiority by beating other kids. We found out later that when their great-grandmother separated them at home they would often redirect their aggression on her. How is it possible to help kids who are so very angry and who do not want to be reached? God gave us the wisdom we needed. We combined the efforts of the adults at Hope Center with the efforts of other kids — multiplying their efforts.

The older boys took on mentoring both brothers. They played with them and they explained what is right and what is wrong and cleaned up together. Jenya and Artyom enjoyed the guidance and started going to them for advice. They began connecting with adults who were overjoyed to see the boys actually defending other kids when someone bullied or offended them. Earlier the boys had ignored everything but now they smiled and participated in dance and song during the Bible lessons. The care, kindness and concern of the adults helped them to realize that they were safe and they no longer had to fight for their lives.

Oleg Kriuko has a similar story but he learned a completely different lesson. After Oleg's father went to jail, his mother became involved with another man who was selling drugs. When his mother would go to work this man would viciously beat Oleg. There was nothing his mother could do without receiving a beating herself.

Finally, Oleg escaped from home and lived on his own for ten months. Through police intervention, he ended up in an orphanage where he felt safe for the first time. Oleg used to have the nickname "the one from the orphanage." This didn't offend Oleg because the orphanage protected him from many hardships. In contrast, "parental love" made him fearful, scared and depressed. At camp he did not strive to dominate, rather he tried to be invisible and not draw anyone's attention. Faced with conflict, he dropped his head and ran. His spirit is broken. It will take many years to restore him and help him understand that nothing is impossible for God!

Oleg always looked forward to hearing bedtime stories read by Mr. Hunt, "the most kind Jim" from Texas. Mr. Hunt's desire was to reach out to every kid's heart. And, he did it! Children can always identify false compassion. Jim was giving real love and kindness that won over the hearts of these children to Christ. Oleg and other boys would hang around Jim's workshop where he was always busy working. They saw that "kind Jim" was always ready to come and offer help to everyone who needed help. Oleg had his heart opened by the touch of God's love. He smiled more often, he talked more, he was no longer confused and asked many questions. Oleg participated in every activity held at the camp. Many times our actions spread the Gospel better than our words.

Yaroslav is a teenager. His tragic story begins at the time of his birth. His mother's pregnancy was without complications, but the doctor who assisted her at birth was drunk and resulted in serious natal trauma for the newborn baby. After three months it became apparent that he would be physically limited. The father could not stand it. Unfortunately, he was not able to love this son who had inherited his looks. He could not accept Yaroslav's physical limitations and abandoned the family. The mother took care of Yaroslav and his older sister by herself. When Yaroslav grew up he could not understand why their father had left them and even blamed himself. Bitterness and a lack of forgiveness overwhelmed him.

This was not the first time Yaroslav came to camp, but this year was special! Having completed seventh grade through a home education program, Yaroslav had grown up a great deal. All year he had looked forward to returning to the camp where he was able to forget how he differs from other kids.

Yaroslav had a hard time going down the hill to the beach and climbing back up the hill. The International Team members and Yaroslav's friends encouraged him during those walks and made it easier for him. He made many new friends at the Hope Center even though for him "friends" is not a simple word. Friends are an opportunity for Yaroslav to communicate, something he does not get enough of since he does not attend school. His best friend was Jim, with whom he talked on different topics during their trips to the beach. Yaroslav likes to dream about the future. Now Yaroslav believes that his dreams can come true! The great God he learned about at the Hope Center has given him hope to find his place in life and to believe in himself.

Alexei from Poltava is 14 years old. He was born in Uzbekistan. His family situation was not a positive one. His father — in and out of prison — was an angry man. He hit his wife freely and was involved with many other women. As war refugees, Alexei's family came to Ukraine when they were forced to leave Uzbekistan. Alexei's mother hoped that with this move to a new country their lives would improve. For a little while life did appear to be better but then his father started to drink again. Once again he began to abuse his wife and returned to his lifestyle of alcohol and promiscuity.

Alexei's mother suffered from a heart condition. His father did not care about her. One day, his father decided that he wanted to kill his wife. He doused her in gasoline and set her on fire, forcing the children to watch. Miraculously, Alexei's mother escaped. One evening, two years after the family came to Ukraine, Alexei's drunken father was hit and killed by a car on his way home from work. This event forced Alexei's mother to seek work sewing and making clothes. In her new job, Alexei's mother met a Christian woman who invited Alexei's family to attend church. Now, Alexei and his mother have been Christians for three years. Soon his mother will have a new husband.

Alexei often thinks about all the different situations in his life. In camp, Alexei asked his counselors and the international team "Why did these things happen in my life?" He asked many questions about God. Alexei gives thanks for all that happened in camp and looks forward to coming back again.

Spiritual Warfare

Where God's work is winning the battle for the hearts and lives of people, Satan is also at work. So, before the arrival of the campers, the International Team fervently pray as they "prayer walk" throughout the camp grounds. They unite as God's soldiers ready to take on the war for these kids. Throughout the camp, team members diligently pray for strongholds to be broken and we see God working in response.

After the first Bible lesson, each child is given a Bible. Like dry sponges soaking in all they can, some of them are excited and ready to accept the teachings. Others ridicule the teachers and have little respect for them. This, however, does not hinder the team and staff. They continue to teach truths that change lives. Each day barriers are broken down. Kids begin to open up. They come up to the stage to participate in songs and skits and listen more intently to the teachings.

In the beginning, counselors struggle to get the kids to take their Bibles to lessons but soon they no longer need to be reminded to bring them. The children begin to read their Bibles with their counselors and even on their own. Bedtime stories become more relaxed with tough questions being asked and more and more kids desiring to pray. We believe this is all due to the power of prayer. Love, attention, understanding and care break down walls in these children's lives.

Chapter 4

GLOMOS - GLOBAL
MODULE STUDIES

IN 1992, AFTER 70 YEARS AS A CLOSED SOCIETY WITH NO religious influence, Ukraine 'opened the doors' to the Good News! For many people, it is fine for them to find their own salvation but the thought of making disciples is still a strange idea. "Why would I worry about others when they are responsible for their own life?"

The country is predominantly Russian Orthodox, a faith in which discipleship is not strong. *Global Action's* training program for pastors and leaders, Global Module Studies (GLOMOS) opens their eyes and sets clear goals in this area.

Only two non-Orthodox denominations survived the Communist era — the Baptists and the Pentecostals. The churches tend to have closed structures and are somewhat distrustful of any other church movements. A spirit of, "I do not know you, I do not want to be with you" is very common among churches. GLOMOS helps to break the barriers between different parts of His body.

GLOMOS enriches the world view of the local churches and people, showing them that there is "a bigger and wider Christianity." There is admiration for the internationalism of the GLOMOS program, the different teachers and the module books written by authors from all over the world. The program helps people to realize the vastness and universalism of Jesus' teaching. GLOMOS provides a certain level of education to people who otherwise would never be able to obtain it. It is especially beneficial to the people from smaller towns and villages.

GLOMOS changes the lives of church leaders and pastors and brings the Good News to remote villages and small towns where it has never been heard before. For the first few years GLOMOS was held at the Ukraine Hope Center. Right now

GLOMOS is held in the northern part of Ukraine, but will no doubt return to the south in the future.

Graduates of GLOMOS are involved in their churches. They launch new prayer groups, new home groups, and new churches. They are more active in "friendship evangelism" and secure in Christian apologetics. Having a good Bible background, they are freer in expressing their beliefs in society and in changing it.

Yuri A. Gulyanytsky is the dean for the GLOMOS program. Yuri was born into a family of well-known musicians in the capital of Ukraine. He is a trained teacher and graduated from Simferopol State University. He later became a school vice-principal. Through his upbringing, he was a good Communist Party member and a good believer in "humanism."

When he was 30 years old, Yuri first heard the Good News in Santa Barbara, California, while involved in a Soviet-American Exchange program visit. Later, in 1991, Yuri met a Korean missionary in his native city of Yalta. He joined the church in 1992, was baptized in 1993, and soon became the pastor's assistant. He served in this capacity until 1997. Yuri also enrolled in Odessa Baptist Seminary for a two-year course of interdenominational studies and received a diploma in Christian Ministry. He was introduced to The Salvation Army in 1997, became a member in 1998, and served as their interpreter in different countries of the former Soviet Union and Europe. At the present time, he serves as the interpreter and teacher with their training college in Moscow.

In 2002, Yuri became acquainted with *Global Action* and has served the ministry in a variety of capacities at summer camps, conferences and GLOMOS. In his current role, Yuri serves as the Academic Dean and as a teacher. His goal is to "firmly establish GLOMOS in my country and to experience teaching it in all the countries where it currently operates."

Yuri: "As a teacher I love to transfer the knowledge I have to people who need and want it. It is important to me to help the people who serve 'on the front lines' to become better equipped for the everyday battle for the hearts of people. It is important for me to see the eyes of those who will take the Good News even further, to assist in their growing and maturing. My heart melts when I hear the words at the end of their sermon which we require them to compose: This is the first time in my life when I am allowed to speak publicly! I have never dreamt of delivering a sermon. Now I will do it as often as I can!"

Igor Grishajev is the administrator for the GLOMOS program. He received Christ as his Savior in 1994. Since that time his life has dramatically changed. In 2004 Igor met with *Global Action* and since then has been working as staff administrator of different projects and as translator. Today he is the program coordinator.

Igor: "I want to arrange and facilitate GLOMOS because it can help Ukrainian pastors transform their lives preparing them to work more effectively in sharing the Good News. GLOMOS unites different denominations in one call— to go and make disciples. What I like in GLOMOS is that it is more important to see lives transformed than just complete a program."

Here are some of the testimonies of the graduates:

Tamara Yurchishina works for The Salvation Army in Beltsy, Moldova. She graduated from GLOMOS in 2007. After her GLOMOS studies she was sent to a church with 67 people. Today the church has a congregation of 120 people.

Nitoumbi Jean Claude is the associate pastor of God's Kingdom, a church in Feodosia, Crimea. He came to GLOMOS in 2006. Studying in the GLOMOS program changed his life. He became a risk-taker who learned how to take responsibility and proclaim God's Kingdom. His expectations came true through GLOMOS and fulfilled his dream to become a pastor. He leads 60 people in the church.

Tamara Mirgorodskaya graduated in 2005. Since that time she has conducted more than 30 theological seminars using the GLOMOS module books. She has trained 70 lay people. In 2006 she recommended Captain Ruslan Zuev to study in the GLOMOS program.

Ruslan Zuev is the pastor of the The Salvation Army church in Yalta, Crimea. He graduated from GLOMOS in 2007. When he came to his new appointment the church had only 13 people.

Today the church has 74 people attending. In GLOMOS, Ruslan learned about *Global Action*'s ministry in India. It became possible for him to join a *Global Action* ministry team going to India in 2007. Since that time he has traveled as a missionary to India several times on his own. There he uses the GLOMOS material to teach lay people. Thirteen of them are now church leaders. He was encouraged by *Global Action* to become a risk-taker. In Ukraine he taught five lay people and three of them are now church leaders.

Irina Reunova graduated in 2005. She has used the GLOMOS books in cell groups, youth groups and in individual training sessions. She taught 10 lay people in her church with the help of the GLOMOS material. Two of them became leaders who were sent to GLOMOS and graduated in 2008.

Sergey is an evangelist who graduated from GLOMOS in 2006. He was the leader of church evangelism at Love of Christ in the city of Krasnoperekopsk, Crimea. In GLOMOS he learned preaching, personal evangelism and how to relate to people. This program has helped him change the way he evangelizes. He added new values learned through GLOMOS into his ministry and is now planting churches. He has planted four churches since he graduated and has taught people using the GLOMOS material in these churches. Six people have become pastors and leaders of the churches.

Artem Domnich is a presbyter of the *City of Light Church* in Simferopol, Crimea. He came to GLOMOS as a prospective leader and graduated in 2005. Redeemed by God, Artem was a drug addict in his past life. On fire for the Lord, GLOMOS was the right program for him. After he graduated from GLOMOS in 2005 he was promoted as a cell group leader. In 2006 he was appointed as the rehabilitation center pastor. Since 2007 he has been an ordained minister and presbyter of the church.

Alexander Alexandrov is the pastor of God's Grace Church. He graduated from GLOMOS in 2008. After GLOMOS he started a new church with 10 people from the village. Today this church has 50 people in the congregation. He uses GLOMOS material to teach the laypeople in his church. GLOMOS prepared him to launch this church and keep it going.

Chapter 5

INTERNATIONAL VOCATIONAL ACADEMY (IVA)

IN UKRAINE AND RUSSIA THERE ARE OVER 650,000 BOYS and girls living in orphanages run by the state. Often these children have ended up in state institutions because both parents are dead, in jail, or because they had so many children they couldn't care for them all. Others are the children of drug addicts or were removed from abusive homes by the state. Millions of others live in homes devastated by drugs, alcohol and marital problems. Their lives have no direction, no role models and no future.

While the children in orphanages have a roof over their head, adequate meals and a relatively safe environment, all that changes when they become 17-years of age. On that birthday — or soon thereafter — children are often walked to the gate of the orphanage and sent on their way. A statistical study shows that within a year 33% are living on the streets, 20% have committed a crime and 10% have attempted suicide.

Just after the New Year 2005 *Global Action* launched a pilot project at the Hope Center with a small group of 16 orphans and underprivileged youth. Similar programs were carried out in 2006 through 2008. Unfortunately, the dip in donor income has made it prohibitive to continue until sometime in the future.

The International Vocational Academy (IVA) is a training program that includes full room and board for the entire length of the program. Participants must agree to complete the full program and must have employable skills to apply. The program is equally focused on developing a transformed, positive, Christian mind-set as well as an occupational skill.

The curriculum includes a basic introduction to the Bible and courses in the Christian faith on renewing your mind, appreciation, servanthood and Christian values. Every week there are feedback sessions as well as individual sessions, conversational English, trade subjects such as Introduction to Computers and Usage (theory and labs), mechanics, woodworking and even house painting. The most sought-after courses are the classes in driving, with the possibility to graduate with a drivers license.

The beginning was not easy. After the first week, one of the students was in court and would have been sentenced to five years in jail. Due to the fact that he was at the Hope Center his jail sentence was reduced to community service.

Some of the boys tested HIV-positive and the young ladies had to be treated for a variety of venereal diseases. There was a lot of teen "ugliness" in the beginning of the program. However, the Lord intervened and we learned many valuable lessons.

The culmination of each IVA program is graduation, a very special event! Suddenly these young men and women are ready to venture out into the real world. These students have lived at the Hope Center for almost six months and have become one big family. It is usually not until just before graduation that they sincerely begin to open up. For some students it was the first time to tell their story and all that they have been going through.

Here are some of the success stories from our IVA programs over the past years.

Sveta graduated in 2005. When she was 16 years old she entered the IVA program in an effort to improve her difficult life. In our program she studied computer skills and economics, but she also received the saving knowledge of Christ. Today Sveta is married and has a young daughter. She and her mother attend a local church. She says that the most important thing she learned at IVA was that she is loved by God. Sveta wants to extend that love and provide the best for her child.

Roman graduated in 2007. He came to us as a young man without many prospects but interested in the opportunity to earn a drivers license through our technical training. He also received instruction in drafting, woodworking, welding, economics, English, computers and Bible lessons.

Today Roman works for the city medical department in Kerch where they have made good use of the skills he learned

Another day... another kind of camp! Young pioneers pose for their camp picture

Young communist pioneers in front of the statue of Lenin

Lenin is coming down!

The cross has conquered Lenin's place!

Andrey soon after his conversion

The happy couple - 2001

Andrey and Tanya Shpigunov
- leaders of the Ukraine Hope Center

Ingegerd and Jörgen Edelgård at the Hope Center cafeteria

East meets West! Sheeba Subhan from the Global Action India staff in training at the Ukraine Hope Center, summer of 2004

Alexander with his new leg together with Ingegerd

Team leader Susanne Griffin-Ziebart discusses the daily camp program with pastor Sergey Frolov

Everyone enters into song at the Morning Devotions

Prayer time is an important event

It is so important to talk to someone willing to listen

Writing a letter to God

Is there a future for me?

*When it is time for bedtime stories, it is good
to have your own Bible ready!*

*Comparing stories from the
Bible.*

Let me tell you what this means!

Getting ready to swim in the Black Sea is special!

Even boys like doing this!

*Zahar having fun
at craft time!*

You can see a lot of smiling faces around the camp!

*IVA students carry out
a school experiment*

*IVA graduation.
A bright future ahead!*

*One of the school programs
teaching abstinence*

*Without the Hope Center
I would go hungry today*

*Denis in his new
wheelchair*

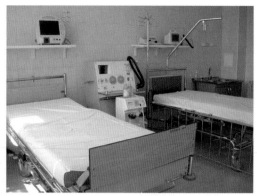

Many of the hospitals in Kerch have been equipped by Global Action

A GLOMOS graduate has just received his diploma from Yuri Gulyanitsky, dean of GLOMOS Ukraine

The Afterschool program makes sure the children do their homework

A girl receives her Christmas box

A hug can sometimes be the best counsel... Tanya comforts a girl

at the Hope Center. He drives a burley 4-wheel drive to transport necessary medical materials and personnel between hospitals and to the homes of those in need.

Artur, who graduated in 2007, studied alongside Roman and also took full advantage of the opportunity to learn a variety of skills. After graduation he stayed at the Hope Center through the summer as a volunteer, cleaning the grounds and helping with camp activities. His attitude, sense of humor and improving English skills made him a popular character with both local staff and the internationals.

In the fall of 2007 Artur went to Moscow for work and did very well. When he returned at the beginning of the summer he was brimming with confidence, ready to take on any challenge. He worked at the Hope Center again in 2008, this time as a security guard. Today he serves as a personal driver and is a frequent visitor to the Hope Center. It was at the Hope Center that he found opportunity and knowledge which he uses to succeed today.

Dima graduated in 2007. He comes from a village just north of Kerch and came to IVA as a means to escape his troubled childhood and self-destructive lifestyle. He took to driving quickly and after his IVA graduation was hired full-time at the Hope Center. He worked with us for 18 months helping with facilities, programs and in the kitchen. In the fall he accepted a job offer from a tool and appliance store in downtown Kerch. He is using his driving skills now in delivering large items to customers all over the Kerch area.

Another Roman graduated in 2008 and has taken advantage of the education he acquired at the Hope Center. We were always impressed by Roman's intelligence and work ethic and knew that he would be able to use his new-found skills well. He quickly received a job with a bread company that is owned by the city of Kerch. When he got the job, he was pleasantly surprised at the good wages that his skills provided. He is now responsible for delivering bread to hospitals, businesses and sometimes even to the Hope Center. He and his girlfriend Yula (also an IVA graduate) visit frequently to keep us updated.

Vlad graduated in 2008 and is from the city of Armyansk in northern Crimea. When he arrived at the Hope Center he instantly became a leader in his class. His English skills, age and maturity made him an integral part of camp life. After graduation he returned home to work temporarily with his stepfather's construction business but soon found a promising position as a truck driver. He now works with his city's electrical department driving the line truck for repairs.

One of the students, Jenya, is 21 years old and came to us from the large industrial city of Krivoy Rog. Upon entering the program Jenya appeared very serious. He was quiet and reserved when talking about himself. Only his documents told of his upbringing in an orphanage. After five months of developing relationships and earning trust he finally began to reveal his story.

Jenya never met his father. His mother told him that his father hung himself before Jenya was born. Alone at 26 years of age, his mother looked to her friends for support but was only introduced to drugs. She quickly became addicted, a habit that she could not break. For a few years she and Jenya lived in a drug house. When she was 36 years old, Jenya's mother died and the ten year old was sent to an orphanage. This was the first time in his life that he had slept in a clean bed, had sufficient food and interacted with other children. After leaving the orphanage he moved to a technical school where many of his friends tried to convince him to use drugs. Having seen what addiction did to his mother, Jenya was strong enough to say "no" to them. He began working 10-12 hours a day as an electrician but his pay was so low that he couldn't afford to pay for food.

Jenya's dream is to continue his education and become a stage actor. At IVA he found hope that he could achieve success beginning with qualifying for a drivers license, new knowledge and Christian principles that he gained. Before he left the Hope Center for Krivoy Rog he told us, "I have learned important life lessons. I met some incredible people who helped me change. I am proud to be an IVA graduate."

Misha was born in an ordinary Kerch family 21 years ago. His mother is a musician and his father moved from job to job to make a living. His father began drinking and smoking excessively. When Misha was only seven years old, his father died of a heart attack. His mother was faced with the tough job of raising her son alone. She had very little income and was forced to have additional jobs to make ends meet.

Misha had nobody to guide him during this time. Looking at his peers, he realized that he would not have the things they had like nice clothes, cell phones, etc. He and his mother could hardly keep bread on their table each day. But his neighborhood friends kept telling him, "There is a chance to have it all. Take it from other people". This is how Misha became a participant in group theft. The court sentenced the shy and thin guy to three years in jail. He was not able to finish the last year of school.

When Misha went to the "Red Prison" he was horrified by the brutality of the prisoners and one of the jailors. For any minor violation of the rules Misha was either beaten or assigned to tough physical labor. He was really shocked by the prison rules. After two years Misha was released due to his diligent labor and gentle behavior. When he returned home he found it difficult to get employed. No one wanted to hire an employee without education and with a criminal past.

Misha's friends tried to get him back into the "business" of stealing, but memories of the years spent in jail blurred all the temptation. Now Misha has mastered driving. He was dreaming about this profession even when he was in prison. But it is only now that his previously unattainable dream is coming true.

When it was time for the Bible courses, ideologies often clashed. The program for Bible lessons is compiled so that the students learn the basic elements of Christianity. About 90% of the IVA students come to us as non-believers and our primary task is to deliver the message that God is real and is able to meet their needs. A few students have had experience with other religions and teachings. Some do not conceal their atheistic outlooks about the creation of the universe. A number of students have also been influenced by Eastern philosophies that have distorted their vision of the world greatly. Some students even brought undisguised occultism with them.

Here is one more powerful story about an IVA student, Alexander Kostylev, who battles Satan and the stronghold Satan has on his mind.

Sasha Kostylev is a rather short young man with a charming smile. When we first met him we could not have imagined the hardships he had endured. In 1998, his 38-year old father died of pancreatic diabetes. His mother was left with two little children. She made very little money at a bakery plant. Sasha was forced to pick up scrap metal and sell it to help the family. When Sasha turned 13 he was also diagnosed with pancreatic diabetes. Doctors said that it was genetic and worsened by the stress of his father's death. During 2001 Sasha was in the hospital 24 times; eight times in the intensive care unit. Doctors did not think Sasha would survive. When he was 16 years old he weighed only 28 kilograms, which is approximately 62 pounds!

Sasha went to Kharkov where he more or less recovered. It was there that he learned about Eastern philosophy from his friend. Impressed with it, he even went so far as to get a tattoo with the ying-yang symbol. Later he learned about the existence of the spiritual world and he made one more tattoo - three 6's on his leg, which in combination with the ying-yang are supposed to mean, "Satan is not going to get me!"

Sasha believes in paradise and hell. He wants to learn more about living Christianity, but his conscience is still closed to God's truth. Too much spiritual garbage has accumulated in his head during the past years. We are sure that Bible lessons and contact with believers will help him to find the way to salvation. We know that our prayers will defeat Satan's strongholds in these young men's lives. Please pray for the IVA students and for their spiritual liberation and salvation.

Chapter 6

AFTER SCHOOL PROGRAM

THE AFTER SCHOOL IS A PROGRAM FOR AT-RISK CHIL-
dren and those who need a safe place to be during the critical
hours of the afternoon. It is focused on boys and girls who are
between the ages of 7 and 12 and who come from extremely
poor or dysfunctional family situations.

The children arrive at the Hope Center between noon and
2 p.m. just in time for a hot, nutritious meal. Before lunch they
are free to play table games or go outside for other activities.
After the children eat lunch they return to their classroom to
complete homework with the help of our staff and volunteers.
This time is also used for individual English tutoring. Once they
complete their class work they have free time until instruction
time begins at 4 p.m. We use this time period for lessons and
lectures in English, Bible, Psychology, rudimentary Economics and other interesting topics. The children are then given a
snack and sent home by 5:30 pm.

During their time at the Hope Center, our resident pediatri-
cian consistently monitors the children's health. Dr. Olga ad-
ministers vitamins and medication as needed. We also provide
coats, clothing and shoes from our humanitarian aid supplies.

In order to fully appreciate the impact of this program it is
essential to know a little about the children who are involved.

Masha is 14 years old. Her parents divorced when she was
ten months old. From that time until she was ten years old,
Masha's mother raised her as a single parent. When Masha was
ten years old her mother disappeared without a trace, leaving
Masha parentless. It is suspected that her mother's frequent
drunkenness may have played a part in her disappearance.
Masha now lives in a rented apartment with her aunt who can
barely support them both on her meager income from selling
fruit.

Masha is frequently sick in the winter. Dr. Olga suspects that it is related to her lack of warm clothes. We allowed her to choose from our selection of high-quality coats from Sweden as well as some warmer clothes and shoes.

Daniel is eight years old. His family life is as tragic as it is confusing. He lives with his grandparents along with seven other children, all of whom are his relatives. He comes to the Hope Center with his uncle Dima who is 12 years old. Dima is also in our program. Daniel's father committed suicide last year and his mother died of a blood disorder. His younger brother is in a small orphanage near the Hope Center because their grandparents cannot afford to raise him. His alcoholic grandfather cannot work as he only has one eye that has very poor vision.

Daniel is a constant challenge. He struggles with his temper and is extremely aggressive towards other children. We are encouraged, though, that we have seen a marked improvement in him within the structure of our program.

Oleg, six years old, is a recent addition to this program. He is the oldest of his mother's children. They all live with the father of the youngest child. Neither his mother nor his stepfather work consistently, and drunkenness is the norm.

Oleg's mother does not want to stay with this man but with three young children to feed she is left with little choice. Oleg is severely stunted in his development. In trying to teach him simple English we learned that he did not even fully understand concepts like numbers, letters, shapes and colors in Russian yet! Dr. Olga has prescribed medication for his chronic bronchitis. His parents are unable and unwilling to have him treated.

Denis, who is 13 years old, is a child from a broken family. His parents divorced when he was two years old. His father subsequently went to prison for robbery. His mother remarried but with an ultimatum from her new husband that she would abandon Denis. She left the three-year-old boy Denis with his grandmother and moved to Israel. She still calls occasionally to talk to him but has no intention of returning for him. Denis still loves his mother very much and faithfully defends her to those who imply that she is a bad mother.

46

Masha's (15) and Vanya's (14) mother had severe diabetes. She had poor circulation in her legs that resulted in one of her legs being amputated. She needed another serious and expensive operation. Their father could not afford it. He was upset about this and was afraid of being alone with the children with his wife so sick. So, he committed suicide. Shortly after this their mother died, leaving the children orphaned.

Then something extremely unusual for Ukraine took place. A neighbor couple, who had no children of their own, decided to adopt Masha and Vanya legally. They lived as a family for one year before the wife left. The husband continued to raise the children on his own. In Ukraine, this is unheard of. Masha tells us that this home situation is very hard sometimes but that she still appreciates it. She is so happy to have a family rather than to live at the orphanage. Someone told the man about our After School program. He submitted applications for Masha and Vanya.

Although Masha and Vanya are older than our target age group (7-12 years old) for the After School program, we still accepted them because of their unique situation. The man tells us that he has seen a huge improvement in the children since they began coming to the Hope Center. Vanya used to disappear for days on end with his friends. Now he is so excited to come to the Hope Center. He is eager to participate actively in all of the activities. Afterwards, he goes home and tells his stepfather stories about all the fun activities he participated in that day.

We recently received new clothes for the children in this program. Masha and Vanya were given some of the warm winter items. They were so happy. Their stepfather struggles to adequately meet the basic needs of his adopted children, including food, education, clothes, and social needs. The gifts that we receive from donors in combination with this program, helps meet the basic needs of the children. They mean so much to this family.

Vera is twelve. Her parents are divorced because her father is an alcoholic. She lives with her mother who cares for her with no support from her father. In addition, Vera's mother is not healthy. Although she does not want to talk specifically about her disease, she explained that she is not able to maintain a full-time skilled job. Instead, she works multiple menial jobs which pay very little and require her to work 18-hour days in order to earn the minimal salary that they need. This means that Vera's mother is rarely at home. Vera understands that the situation is difficult for her mother so she tries to be good.

Vera works hard at school and performs very well. Vera's mother was so thankful that Vera could be in this program because she knew that here Vera will be safe and surrounded by good people, do her homework and receive one full meal a day. It means that Vera will not have to be alone so much. Vera's favorite activities at the Hope Center are the English classes with our intern Judith. When Vera came home with items from the packages sent by kind women, her mother wrote a letter to the Hope Center. She described how thankful she is that Vera received the new clothes and how grateful and surprised she is that Vera can receive all of this for free.

Nadia (13), Vika (11), and Kolya (8) all live with their mother and away from their father because he is an alcoholic. When he is drunk he often beat Nadia, Vika, Kolya, and their mother. Finally, their mother took the three of them and escaped to an apartment. The apartment has no heating system. When it is cold, they set up a little tent inside their home and make a small fire with a few pieces of wood. The family has a rule that whoever comes in first must make the fire. It does not provide much heat. Surviving only on the mother's salary, the family only has enough money for some food.

The children were very excited to receive some new clothes from the packages sent by a generous group of women. When Kolya put on his camouflage coat for the first time he beamed with delight and posed in it with pride. Before receiving a sweatshirt he only had one thing to wear. Kolya said he will save the new sweatshirt for special occasions like an important exam that he will take at school soon.

Nadia, Vika, and Kolya just love to be at the Hope Center. They want to be here as much as possible and do not want to go home at the end of the school day. Often they ask if we can organize some activities on the weekend as well. They especially look forward to the hot meals and eat huge amounts of food during lunch, much more than the other children. The cooks know where these children sit and put extra food on their table. Usually, they take bread home in their pockets. They are even more excited about the sweet snacks, a treat they would never receive at home.

During the Bible lesson one day, Kolya wrote a letter to God. At the end of the letter he asked God to help him study well, to be rich and have enough money for food, clothes and a warm home. Their mom is extremely thankful that her children have the opportunity to be in a warm place with full stomachs and around good people. When facing difficult times and struggling to provide for her children their mom wonders if they would be better off in an orphanage. She realizes that having support and resources through the After School program helps her to keep her children. In this way, the program not only helps children but also their parents, while minimizing the number of children in orphanages.

One of our counselors shares her perspective. "Although it is not always easy, working with these children is a great opportunity to serve each other, to show unconditional love and enduring patience through the roller coaster ride of emotions and behaviors. It is a privilege to share in their happiness and sadness, to feel and understand the emotions that they are feeling and to provide comfort or advice in the situations they are facing. Even helping them with homework that may seem to them so difficult is rewarding. We take care of them in ways their parents, lacking resources or time, may not be able to: offering a shower, washing their clothes or shoes, or doing their hair nicely. At the same time, as counselors we must enforce necessary rules in a loving Christian way. This creates an environment where the children also learn discipline and obedience. These children need the guidance and instruction that an adult who loves them provides. We always strive to introduce ways to help the children learn something new on their own and to find activities to keep the program interesting and fun for them. This kind of job brings us back to our childhood, never lets us be bored, and prevents us from worrying about our own problems."

We know that this is an important program. But the true impact it has on each child's life does not become apparent until trust is developed and the kids begin to open up and share a bit about their lives. This is often difficult for them to do.

Chapter 7

THE STREET CHILDREN

SINCE 2006, *GLOBAL ACTION* HAS BEEN CARRYING OUT A project called Street Kids. During our Christian summer camps we met several kids living in dysfunctional families. Some of the kids privately told us about the difficulties they have had to face each day, such as the lack of food, drunken parents, physical and sexual violence which forces them to leave their families and to become homeless. This inspired us to create a new program. Street Kids not only refers to homeless children, but to those living in dysfunctional families as well.

The Street Kids project is being carried out through several avenues: (1) Providing meals at churches and schools situated in poor neighborhoods; (2) Equipping kids with clothes and school supplies; (3) Educating parents on issues of raising children and their legal responsibilities as a parent.

At the present time we stay in touch with five families by providing them with informative material on raising children. Teachers agree that this program is very valuable. It provides children with hot food at least once a week and shows them that they are cared for.

As often as possible members of the Hope Center staff travel to one of the local churches for a feeding program. The charity meals attract between 10 to 15 children ranging from three to 15 years old. We have become close friends with these kids.

Maksim and Ivan are brothers. Their father is 32 years old and is a non-functional alcoholic. For several years he has not been working. Their mother works at a railway-switch factory. Her job is very challenging and tough. The money she makes is scarcely enough to support the whole family.

The boys spend most of their time outside because their father is continually beating them. Their mother cannot afford to buy the boys new clothes so they have to wear their father's used clothes. When they received the clothes brought to them from the Hope Center, the boys were extremely happy. Like adults, they picked the clothes they needed most.

We have known the Glinskiy girls for several years. They attend charity meals and they also study at the Winds of Change program at the Hope Center. This program includes free courses in English and computer skills. It was very exciting for the sisters to receive new clothes. By Ukrainian standards their family is below the poverty line.

Sasha and Natasha Dunayev live in a small village called Ivanovka. They are twins and go to a school that is located 20 km (12 miles) away from their home. The kids live in a remote house that is not suitable for living. They live with their parents who are constantly drinking alcohol. Their parents only leave the house to get money to buy alcohol. Sasha and Natasha walk around the village hoping to find help. The girls are very excited each time they receive fruit brought to them weekly by "kind people." One of our team members, Christine Roderick, has regularly been sending clothes, school supplies and candy for the children and this has had a great positive influence on their mother.

Vanya Teterin is seven. His parents abandoned him. He lives with his grandmother and an 18-year-old aunt. Every Friday Vanya looks forward to meeting members from the Hope Center. For him it is the only chance to enjoy a banana or an orange and to have some juice. They live on his granny's tiny retirement payment, hardly enough to keep them from starving. His 18-year-old aunt came to pick up some clothes — sent here by *Global Action* — for Vanya.

The Kursky family is large. There are seven children from different fathers varying from two to 15 years of age. Four of the children go to the village school where our feeding program is held. The mother is an alcoholic and her new husband provides for the family by selling scrap material.

Their living conditions are horrible. The children come to school untidy, dirty, hungry and sometimes with bruises on their faces. They were so happy when members of *Global Action* came to their house and brought food for their family. There was no end to their happiness when they received Christmas gifts.

The Katalupovs live in the Mayak village. For five years Tatyana, the mother, has been ill with tuberculosis. She has three children and they are very poor. Because there are minimal job opportunities in the village, the mother works hard for very little pay. The money she makes is only enough to buy medicine for her and some food for her children. People who know about their problems share clothes with them. Two of her children — Yulia and Kolya — attend the school where *Global Action* provides the feeding program for poor and large families. Their mother is very grateful that her children can receive hot food because she is not always able to provide them with a hearty lunch.

There are many more children and families throughout these villages that are in need. Although the children live in families, they continue trying to survive in tough conditions just like the street kids.

Chapter 8

AROUND KERCH

AROUND KERCH INCLUDES ACTIVITIES CONDUCTED by the Hope Center staff and volunteers but takes place outside of the Hope Center boundaries. We have highlighted five surrounding villages and on-going projects such as distribution of clothes and shoes, wheelchairs and walkers for the physically challenged, feeding programs for hungry children and humanitarian aid to the needy. We also provide informational presentations in the village schools educating on issues such as drugs, alcohol, smoking, human trafficking and HIV/AIDS.

After distributing questionnaires in the villages we learned what the community saw as the most serious social problems: 94% of the residents responded that alcohol was a major problem; 42% reported that drugs were a major issue; and 7% point toward HIV/AIDS.

Using this information to create a specialized presentation for the village, *Global Action* expanded the Around Kerch program. We first talked with 40 students over the age of 12 about alcohol abuse and provided a booklet that outlines the dangers of alcoholism. The students then invited their friends, families and neighbors to a larger meeting.

We presented the same lecture in the village of Chistopolye to a group of 120 people. We did not have enough seats inside the hall so we were forced to do the same lecture for those seated outside. A forum at which attendees could voice concerns, ask questions and suggest solutions followed the presentation.

We have continued to present the same programs in other villages around Kerch in an effort to have greater reach and effectiveness in the communities where we work.

In 2010 we launched *Around Kerch-2*, to address one of the largest problems in our nation. Using alcohol is a huge risk factor that negatively affects our health. This problem is not only with individuals but now it destroys lives and separates families. The World Heatlh Organization reports that the European nation with the highest level of teenage alcoholism, at 40% of teenagers, is Ukraine.

In one year, forty thousand people died because of alcohol in the country. Ukraine has two million alcoholics. One-and-a-half milion children live in alcoholic family situations. Eighty percent of crimes are committed by people under the age of 35 who carried them out under the influence of alcohol. Teenagers can buy alcohol very easily in Ukraine due to low prices and the sale of alcohol to underage teenagers. Usually, teenagers do not understand the risk and even lack information about alcohol, its consequences, and its influence on them. This places teenagers in a high-risk zone.

In our project *Around Kerch-2*, we address these issues of alcohol through a variety of methods, including seminars, training sessions, and focus groups. In the focus groups, we have the opportunity to build friendships with teenagers and to get to know them personally. We can see their needs, watch how their relationship with alcohol changes, and see how alcohol plays a role in other problems in their lives. Our main goal is to show alternatives, to show new and better examples, and to destroy stereotypes in our society.

We are grateful for the grants from Sweden that made this project possible.

Chapter 9

PROJECT CARE

SUNDAY. A SPECIAL DAY! FAMILIES USUALLY SPEND time together talking, enjoying much needed rest and making time for each other. This is only possible when you are part of a family.

How do children who live in orphanages spend their Sundays? Some kids who live in the Kerch orphanage are never taken home by relatives on the weekends. Sunday is just another day in the orphanage, sometimes with the treat of a walk. Sadly, the children are bored on a day that should be a special day. Naturally, these children grow envious of those with loved ones, wishing they had the same privilege.

In an effort to change this situation, we decided to visit the children in the orphanage on Sundays, and bring them a little joy. This is how the project Care came into existence. We are convinced that it is a necessary program that must continue. We cannot leave the children without attention and love.

The primary focus of this care has been furthering social adaptation, providing educational materials and psychological support, promoting healthy life-styles and introducing Christian values. During some of the weekends, the children participate in a "Day-Off Club" where various activities are planned for them. For the junior age children we focus on outside recreation, table games, fun exercises, singing, crafts, cartoons and movies that introduce Christianity and Christian values. For the senior students the focus is more on debates and discussion clubs on important youth problems, documentary films and movies with positive messages, entertaining projects, hiking, concerts, as well as an educational course in Christian ethics.

This new project format provides the Hope Center with a better platform to speak with kids of various ages and attract new volunteers from different churches to work with the children from the orphanages.

During the past school year, Care continued its activities. Simple visits with sweets and small gifts contribute to the children's sense of self-worth. Volunteers Nina, Marina, Judith, and Chris spent time interacting with the children. The time spent together was beneficial and put to good use by reading Bible stories and discussing serious topics like "my future profession," "human trafficking" and "hygiene." The girls enjoyed this time to talk—over a cup of juice—about the urgent issues of life or about how the day went. A favorite part of these visits was craft time—always out of the ordinary and interesting—especially when doing it in the company of friends!

Counselors in the orphanage always comment on how the children look forward to Sunday, a day when they communicate with friends and learn something new. For the volunteers, working in this project is an opportunity to serve using their talents, skills, and love.

Marina is one of the volunteers. She loves to think up crafts. "I get enormous pleasure from working with the children in Project Care. We made different crafts, communicated with each other and learned to interact with the children. The girls told me about how they are doing in school, what is going on in their lives and their concerns. I am glad to see how they change and have grown more open. I am glad that I can help them and develop good friendships. I think that these friendships will continue and that we will continue to help each other. From these interactions, I understand that family is very important. Nothing can substitute for having a warm and loving family life. In an orphanage, it is difficult to fill this void. But, you can give emotional warmth, share your love, and show them that they are needed and important. They are now in my heart. I pray that not one of them will be lost from God."

Nina is a counselor and creates the lessons on urgent themes and Bible topics. "To work with children from the orphanage through the Project Care is a huge blessing for me. Throughout the year, I see the children's perspective of life and view of God change. For example, they came to understand the importance of studying, having a profession, and being independent in life. I understand how important it is to pray about families that deprive their children of the opportunity to live at home, receive warmth and be loved by parents and close ones. I pray that the project may continue so that we can continue to give the children what they need."

Judith is a volunteer who participates in everything. She helps with crafts, photography and provides transportation by being the driver. "These precious girls so desperately desire hugs, love and attention. Even the girls who did not yet know us would run to us for hugs as though we were old friends. Often, the little girls would have visible cuts or bruises. Although these things are normal for active kids, the counselor told of how they fight with each other—like boys—because of a small argument. This problem solving method seems to have been learned from their past experiences. They truly need positive role models and healthy examples of adult women in their lives – people to learn from and look up to. As we worked on crafts, played games and shared Bible stories, the girls were always so eager to learn and participate. They took pride in everything they created and learned. With even the smallest little gifts that we gave them—ranging from a pen to a Christmas shoebox gift—the girls cherished each item. Through this experience, I can now see how necessary genuine love shown in simple ways is for these children. This program offers just that: genuine love shown through the simple act of being present in their lives."

Here are some of the children's stories:
Since the age of five, Jenya has lived in the orphanage. Her parents are both alcoholics. When her neighbors heard her crying and saw that her parents did not care for her they brought Jenya to the orphanage. In the beginning, some relatives came to visit Jenya occasionally. Now, nobody visits her. Nobody is interested in Jenya.

Yulya is ten years old. Although she is very kindhearted, Yulya is sensitive and distrustful as a result of her mother and father's betrayal. Her only visitor is her grandmother and those visits do not happen very often. Yulya prays for her relatives and asks the Lord for a warm house where she will live with her mother.

Ksusha is also ten years old. Because her parents left her at the orphanage and then disappeared, Ksusha now lives there.

Everybody, except her grandmother who sometimes invites Ksusha to her home, forgot about her entirely. Unfortunately, when her grandmother brings Ksusha to her home to visit in the springtime, she uses her to earn money by making Ksusha sell flowers in the marketplace. Yet, Ksusha remains a cheerful girl, bubbly about life. She likes to smile and is very kind. Ksusha prays to God that He will come into the hearts of her mother and father.

When we met this eight years old girl in the orphanage, we were excited to hear her wonderful rare name – Avgusta. She was playing with her friends and did not differ much from the other kids in the group in any way, neither by her looks, nor by her behavior. There was an obvious deep sadness in her eyes that drew us to her. When watching cartoons we noticed that every scene with aggression towards people or animals provoked the girl's deep emotions. She would start to cry and then go to her room and isolate herself.

Social workers said Avgusta had experienced much abuse growing up. Her mother was fifteen years younger than her father. He would often beat both Avgusta and her mother and then kick them out of the home. When Avgusta was two years old, her mother brought her to an orphanage to protect the girl from her father's sadistic acts. But in two weeks he came to the orphanage and made her take off her new clothes, put on her old clothes and took her back home.

Time passed. The social worker often visited the girl's home but nobody would open the door. A neighbor shared what had been going on in that "horrible flat." They could hear a girl's harrowing shouts; a lady's cries asking for help, swearing, abuse and crashing of plates. The police did not react initially. When they finally intervened, it was too late. A physician examined Avgusta and discovered that she had many bruises and scarring. They testified that her father systematically raped the girl over several years. He was convicted to many years in prison. However, the mother was missing after the court trial and so Avgusta was brought back to the orphanage.

The pain Avgusta experienced cannot be expressed by words. To describe the depth of the wounds inside her young, tender soul is not possible. The staff at the Hope Center wants to embrace her with the healing love of Jesus Christ and restore her to a happy childhood without further damage or loss.

Chapter 10

AND THEN IT WAS CHRISTMAS

CHRISTMAS TIME IS COMMONLY KNOWN AS A TIME TO be joyful, to give and receive gifts, and to spend time with those who are special to us. For some, this time of the year is no different than any other time: lonely, joyless, and hopeless. Every January *Global Action* holds its annual Children's Christmas Festival in Kerch. We expanded the program to allow 3,000 orphans and underprivileged children to join us during one of three separate events!

The primary objective of this festival is to tell children about the true meaning of Christmas, emphasizing and reminding everyone present of eternal values: mercy, compassion, and helping our fellow man. The highlight of this program includes the presentation of a gift to each child.

Children came from Kerch and the surrounding villages for an entertaining Christmas play performed by local actors and some of our own staff and volunteers. *Global Action* provided bus transportation for the children.

We also welcomed a number of children brought by the City Department for Disabled Children. All who attended were given a shoebox gift provided by our partner organization in Scotland, *Blythswood Care*. Each shoebox included an excellent mix of practical and whimsical gifts, delighting both children and parents.

Representatives from the city government visited to observe this unique event and were extremely impressed with both the organization and distribution of gifts. The festival was covered by the local newspaper and the city's official news website. Even our local TV station interviewed several of our staff members and volunteers.

One year, a talented group of children and adults from the concert group Emmanuel presented a musical and theatrical performance of "*The Old Boot Maker.*" In this story, a grandfatherly man eagerly awaits the coming of Jesus on Christmas Eve night. This performance beautifully portrays the gospel message of serving Jesus by offering food, drink, clothing, and friendship to those in need.

The singing performances, the brightly decorated stage, the heartfelt songs, and the unique story could leave no viewer feeling indifferent. Some even left the performance moved to tears. Following this performance, a surprise showing of a cartoon film, "Christmas of Spanky," left the children applauding the happy ending to the adventures of a little puppy named Spanky.

Volunteers took great care to ensure that each gift reached the child for whom it was especially prepared. In total, 35 volunteers worked selflessly to carry boxes, distribute gifts, organize the festival, and socialize with the children and their parents. During the festival, more than 3,000 gifts were given away!

What about the children who could not come to the festival? *Global Action*'s desire is to bring as much joy as possible to those who need it most so we decided to bring gifts to the homes of children who are physically challenged, especially those who are housebound. When visiting their homes, it is almost impossible to look at the children with a genuinely happy face – instead you feel such pity.

These children do not need our pity! These precious children need love, hope, and joy, all of which they receive through your prayers and gifts. Bringing these gifts to these children is such a privilege and a blessing. The blessing multiplies when they open their door to us. Some families also opened their hearts and shared their stories.

Sasha is 16 years old. When he was ten years old, he began losing muscle strength in his legs, making it difficult for him to move. This muscle atrophy was due to a genetic disorder and progressed to the point that he could not move his legs at all. As a result Sasha was confined to a wheelchair. Although his parents hope that the disorder will stop progressing, it continues to worsen each year. Now, it has progressed to his arms. Because he cannot travel to school, he studies at home. His apartment is located on the second floor of a building with no elevator, making coming and going very difficult.

Despite his physical handicap, Sasha is very motivated to learn and accomplish great things. He has already created a computer presentation about our city's history. His dream is to attend a university and study computer programming.

Ivan is an eight-years-old who was born with cerebral palsy. He is severely physically and developmentally handicapped. He almost never talks in spite of his mother's attempts to teach him a few letters. He spends most of his time lying on his bed under the care of his mother and grandmother. Although he is able to move his legs spastically and crawl, he cannot walk. With such minimal muscle strength and poor coordination, Ivan falls a lot, leaving his tiny body covered with bruises.

As a result of problems that occurred during his birth, Vadim has cerebral palsy. He is 19 years old and unable to use his arms and legs or leave the confines of his bed. His grandmother is his primary caregiver and recalls that he has had so many operations—including one in Hungary—that they have lost count. All of the operations were unsuccessful. Vadim's spine remains so severely curved that he can only lie on one side. He never developed the ability to speak.

In an effort to educate him, Vadim's family reads books to him and then leaves them propped open at the bedside for him to continue looking at the pictures. His parents work very hard to pay for his medications. They dream of somehow getting Vadim a special bed that will make his life more comfortable and help him be more functional.

Three days after being born healthy and while still in the maternity hospital with his mother, Ilya experienced something horrific. The nurse dropped him. His heart stopped beating. A good doctor saved his life by reviving his heart but before the doctor could revive his heart, Ilya's brain suffered significant oxygen deprivation which added to the brain damage.

While being transported to a better hospital for rehabilitation, Ilya's heart stopped a second time. Again, the doctor revived him. Now, Ilya has cerebral palsy and is severely mentally and physically handicapped with no chance for recovery. At times, he communicates through simple signs. His only words are "Mama" and "Papa." Although his mother believes he retains a little sight—his eyes respond to light and movement—Ilya is blind. His mother hopes desperately for improvement and seeks any available rehabilitation opportunities. During rehabilitation in Simferopol his arm was accidentally broken. He then received further rehabilitation in Kerch for this injury. As Ilya's mother shared his story, she was not able to fight back the tears.

It is difficult to hear and tell the stories of the realities of these children but we believe it is the only way we can know how to pray for our brothers and sisters in Christ. These are the ones Jesus called us to serve. We are so glad that God has allowed us to be His instruments!

Chapter 11

HUMANITARIAN AID

EVERY YEAR THE HOPE CENTER RECEIVES A MINIMUM of six trucks from the Salvation Army's Humanitarian Aid Department in Sweden. *Global Action* graciously pays the freight costs for these trucks.

This humanitarian aid is distributed to three main areas: government-run enterprises (like hospitals and schools); municipal and charitable organizations (like the Red Cross and the Fire Department); and, specific individuals (such as the physically disabled, abandoned senior citizens, the poor and those involved in the projects operated by the Hope Center).

A large percentage of these items go to local hospitals and medical offices and makes it possible for them to provide for our community. The most recent truckload was distributed to five area hospitals, including maternity and mental hospitals. Items such as beds, linens, walkers, wheelchairs, furniture and much more are provided in order to increase the comfort and quality of care in these institutions.

Currently, *Global Action* is the only organization in Kerch that shows its commitment to help challenged people by its actions, not only with words. The medical facilities that receive this equipment are very grateful for the help, because the equipment improves the quality of their work with patients and makes it possible to save hundreds of human lives.

The Hope Center is also a beneficiary of these humanitarian aid items. In fact, the camp is almost entirely outfitted with items from these shipments. From the beds in the wards to the desks in the offices to the tables and chairs in the dining hall and the dishes in the kitchen, the Hope Center has been greatly blessed by these aid shipments.

The most rewarding aid is that which is distributed to individuals in the local community. Kerch and the surrounding villages have a great deal of need. We are pleased to be able to provide necessary items to many local citizens. Recently we distributed wheelchairs to several people from our area.

Here are their stories.

Sergey was born in Gorky, Russia, and is 77 years old. He entered the Soviet Army in 1953 and became a paratrooper. He was released after breaking his leg on a parachute jump. The leg never healed correctly, causing Sergey daily pain and is getting worse year by year. Last year he heard about *Global Action.* We were able to provide him with a walker. While this was a great help, with the extent of pain he endured, it proved to be insufficient. This year we offered to replace his walker with a wheelchair. Sergey gladly accepted, thanking us for our continued attention and care for his situation.

Denis is only ten years old and comes from Kerch. When he was born, he appeared to be a healthy baby, but when he turned four the doctors noticed that he suffered from flat feet. At six he was diagnosed with muscular dystrophy. Because he is not mobile his teachers must come to his home for his education. His mother tried unsuccessfully for over a year to save enough money to purchase a wheelchair for Denis. She brought Denis to the Hope Center when she heard that we help people with needs like his. We were able to outfit him with a chair that they never could have purchased on their own. Now Denis has a level of mobility and normalcy that he has not had in years.

Jenya is a 16-year-old boy from Kerch. He has been physically challenged since birth. In spite of his physical limitations, Jenya is energetic, clever and an avid reader. One day he hopes to become a film producer. He was not able to visit the Hope Center to receive a wheelchair so our staff brought one to his home.

Jenya dreams of being able to walk and play with his friends one day. He continues to see doctors in Simferopol and Donetsk and truly believes that he will overcome his disability. When we gave him his new chair Jenya told us, "Thank you so much for the wheelchair. It will help me so much but someday I hope to give it back!"

Elena has been physically challenged since childhood when she suffered a spinal injury. She is now 49 years old. Like Denis, she was educated at home due to her lack of mobility. Elena did not let this stop her from learning. She now makes a living as an English tutor. Her students must come to her for their lessons. Elena received a chair and is convinced that this will change her life. She can now lead a more active life and be a better, more successful tutor since she is no longer confined to one room in her home.

Within four months of her daughter's birth, Tatiana was completely paralyzed in both legs leaving her bound to a wheelchair. In 2003, she underwent surgery to return the use of her legs but the operation was unsuccessful. More advanced surgeries are available in the capital city of Kiev, however the cost is prohibitive for her family. Tatiana expressed to *Global Action* that she dreamt of having a computer so that she could help her husband in supporting the needs of their family. *Global Action* was finally able to supply her with her own computer. Before receiving this computer, Tatiana felt helpless. Now she has a purpose and a way to give back to her family.

Maria Goncharenka, originally from the country of Moldova, moved to the small village of Chistopolia 50 years ago. She worked very hard at the train station while raising her son and daughter on her own.

Both children have made poor decisions, abusing alcohol and never getting along with each other or their long-suffering mother. The daughter began using drugs and became so depressed that she later committed suicide. Her son is still alive and continues to live with her, but he has become very abusive and often beats her. The violence is so bad that sometimes she is forced to find somewhere else to sleep. Last winter Maria even had to sleep outside a few times because her home is not a safe place for her.

Gala, who is working for the Hope Center, heard of Maria's story and began searching for help. *Global Action* supplies humanitarian aid to a hospital in Bagerovo, a neighboring village to Maria's. Gala pleaded for someone from this hospital to personally go to Maria and bring her medicine and clothing.

Gala and Jenya also continue to take food to her once a week, talk to her about Jesus, and invite her to attend the local church in her village.

Stories of the people we have met during the distribution of wheelchairs can be united under a single phrase — "When misfortune was least expected."

Sasha Gorshenin, a young man of 27 years, is full of life and energy, but Sasha cannot move without assistance. When he was a soldier his spinal column was injured during military exercises. All of Sasha's plans were crushed. The good people around him supported him and taught him a new way to live. Sasha accepted Jesus in his heart. One of the Swedish humanitarian shipments provided Sasha with a wheelchair that allows him to take advantage of new opportunities.

The Musaevs, a family of Crimean Tartars, could hardly wait for the birth of their first child. When their son was born they were very happy. However, very soon the doctors discovered a frightening diagnosis — cerebral spastic infantile paralysis. The new parents spent all their money and expended great effort to help their child. Their efforts were in vain. Now Absetar is 13 years old.

The Government cannot provide enough wheelchairs for physically challenged people, even those who can afford to purchase them. When Absetar's parents found out about *Global Action* and the aid it gives to physically disabled people, they could not believe that in our country this was for real. Later, when they received a wheelchair for free, they were immensely grateful for the people who give physically challenged people the joy of movement and a chance to live a normal life.

We are thankful that we are able to meet some of the physical needs of these people with the resources that have been donated to the Hope Center. It is our hope and prayer that as we continue to distribute aid items in the local communities that we will have even more opportunities to impact lives and exemplify Christ's love.

Chapter 12

YOUR LIFE - YOUR CHOICE

THERE IS GREAT URGENCY TO CREATE A HEALTHY NA-
tion in Ukraine. The average life span of a Ukrainian is less
than 60 years. Research shows that this dismal data is the result of the Ukrainian lifestyle. Excessive smoking, alcoholism,
drugs and insufficient sexual education exert a devastating influence over health and lead to premature death. Special attention should be paid to the under aged — ages 10 to 16 — who
are on the threshold of adult life. Their lifestyle and behavioral
models are just being shaped.

This data is the basis for the project *Your Life Is Your Choice*
launched by the Hope Center. The project carries out educational activities and promotes a healthy lifestyle.

A series of lectures has been prepared on different subjects:
Problems of addictions in a contemporary community; Beer alcoholism – a real threat; Smoking Tobacco (movie); Prisoner of
illusions (drug addiction); What you should know about AIDS-
infection; Abortion- the consequences of a premature sex life;
Sexually transmitted diseases; Modern slavery (human trafficking): myth or reality, as well as computer dependence and
Child Cruelty.

Our activities are not limited to multimedia lectures. Or-
ganizing sports competitions for the youth at the Hope Center
and at schools has become a good tradition in our city. This
program has become another strong brick in building the foundation of a healthy Ukraine.

School principals are pleased with *Your Life Is Your Choice*.
Alexander Gribov, school Principal at the Mayak village tells
us, "We are very glad that there is an organization which is
able to come to our remote countryside school to present lectures on prevention of such asocial phenomena as alcohol, drug
addiction and tobacco use among the youth. Governmental or-

ganizations working with youth seldom come to our school for lectures. The situation in the village is very serious. Young men drink alcohol and the number of those taking drugs constantly increases. I am very concerned with this issue. That is why I consider this project vital for our children and us. We must use every opportunity to protect our kids from these dangers and addictions."

Svetlana Ovsyannikova, Vice-principal at the Priozyornoe village school. "In our school these lectures have been presented since January. They have informed the school children about HIV/AIDS, drug addiction and we watched a film about smoking, *The Bitter Truth*. Teenagers are not always eager to listen to lectures because they think they know everything. However, we have another situation here — senior students are always looking forward to listening to these lectures; they really want to be there. It is too early to speak about results, but teachers have noted that some children have already changed their attitude towards their health. This is obvious, given that the group of smokers behind our school has decreased by three times. This is exciting! Thank you for helping to change the attitude of our kids towards their health and for influencing their outlook."

Svetlana Dudarenko has been a principal in Bagerovo since 1982. "I have been the principal for more than 25 years. What is happening with our youth now is really horrible! Kids start smoking and drinking alcoholic beverages at 7 and 8-years of age. This can be attributed to several factors: Parents drink alcoholic beverages; Kids are not involved in any extracurricular activities like sports and handicrafts; and, children lack support and positive control from parents. All these factors result in acute problems. Teachers offer activities in an attempt to prevent these serious issues among the kids. Unfortunately, the students are used to us. We are only their teachers. We consider ourselves teachers and friends who really want to help, who they trust and listen attentively to. Some of our senior students decided to write a drama about fighting addictions and performed it for the junior students. They were so impressed by your lecture. We hope for further cooperation from our students."

Chapter 13
WITH YOU

THE MAIN TARGET GROUP OF THE WITH YOU PROGRAM is girls who grow up at boarding-type orphanage schools, called an internat. The activities of *With You* are directed at the senior students who attend the internat and the girls who have already graduated.

At the age of 17 the majority of the girls leave the internat and continue their studies at a state vocational school where professions such as hairdresser, chef, train conductor, etc., are taught. The girls are living in "government" housing complexes. The setting of these housing complexes and the conditions are very similar to what you would see and what the girls experience at the internats, with the exception that there is no staff available to supervise them.

Consequently, the girls live with several people in one room, poor heating and inadequate bathroom facilities. Almost all higher education has a monetary fee and grants or loans are few or not available at all. It is very difficult for any youth from this environment to continue on to higher education. Students receive no guidance from the internat staff, and wishes or goals are seldom part of the focus in any discussion.

Statistical data shows that approximately 70% of the girls graduating from the internat fall victim to prostitution. The prostitution takes place at the housing complex and on the streets.

The perpetrators are boys who live at the complex and men from the streets. Students live at these housing complexes along with people who cannot afford apartments. This increases the risks for these girls. There are several obvious reasons behind the high instance of girls falling victim to prostitution but the most important one is low self-esteem and economic hardship. Other contributing factors are drug abuse, threat of violence and peer pressure. Without adequate supervision the girls engage in sexual promiscuity with boys. In return, the girls are paid a small amount of money that provides income for personal needs like new clothes. The strong bureaucracy in this country also works against these girls. They are seldom aware of their rights as an individual and do not know what authority to turn to in order to receive help.

The overall project goal for *With You* is to decrease the number of girls from internats and orphanages who fall victim to prostitution and increase their opportunity to live fufilled lives.

More specifically, an important objective is to increase the alternatives available for these girls, preparing them to provide for themselves. This will have viable effects on decreasing poverty among them.

The high instances of early pregnancy is common in this group of young people and will affect the next generation. Due to their financial situation and the lack of support from the community, the children born to unwed mothers are often placed in institutions. By improving the situation for the girls the possibility of keeping their children will be greatly increased.

To carry out this project, the Hope Center has qualified for government grants from the Swedish government. We believe that through positive relationships we can encourage these young women to discover a new way to live. The curriculum deals with vitally important topics such as: self-worth; medical effects of early sexual activity; abortion; AIDS/HIV; careers and professions; good personal hygiene; sexually transmitted diseases; prenatal care and mothering; learning to say "no" without guilt; alcohol, drugs and smoking addictions; human trafficking and prostitution; and marriage. We were extremely thorough in creating our curriculum and assembling the materials. The finished product is of such quality that we have already received requests from local teachers to use our materials.

Currently, we are training and mentoring over 100 girls with another 40 girls on a waiting list who wish to participate. We were very intentional in our selection of the girls who would enter the program. Recruiting efforts centered on current or past residents of orphanages and internats, college students and girls from the surrounding villages.

Not all of those invited to participate are currently involved in prostitution, but many are. The rest may be soon without dramatic intervention. Of specific concern is the effort to give these girls a viable vocation that can sustain them and provide them with an alternative to prostitution. We help them explore options for education and career paths and aid them in pursuing a planned course.

The grant we received from Sweden also provided for advertising to raise awareness of the issues connected to prostitution. We were able to rent billboards in strategic locations around town - specifically where younger people are likely to see them. We also placed a video spot on local television and on a video advertising board in two supermarket locations.

During the first focus group meetings the girls completed a general questionnaire concerning the topics that would be covered in the curriculum. More than 80% of those in attendance responded that they would like to work in another city or country. The respondents stated that salary levels are highly important while only 50% believed that human trafficking was a major issue. The top three responses to the question of why women resort to prostitution were: bad role models, lack of money and lack of understanding the consequences. These responses make sense. Our program is designed to deal with all three causes.

The mentors report that the importance of this program is even more necessary than they could have imagined. Many of the girls had never been instructed in personal hygiene. In addition, the problem of sexual promiscuity has been a major topic because it is already a normal part of their lives. Please pray for these young women as they work towards discovering a healthier and more fulfilling lifestyle than the one towards which they are heading.

Chapter 14

MAKING THE
HOPE CENTER WORK

IT TAKES MORE THAN BUILDINGS TO RUN THE HOPE
Center! It takes people. Right now we have 14 full-time people
year around and another 21 people who work part-time, especially during the summer months.

We would have a problem managing all the camps without the help of our interns. These volunteers are young people
and senior people coming to give several months of their time
serving with us. Some of them come for the winter months and
help out with all the various projects. Summer teams come to
minister to the children. Without them we would not be able to
put on such festive, energizing summer camps for these disadvantaged children.

However, nothing would work if it had not been for the
work teams – men and women who have come spring and fall
to ensure that the Hope Center is well-maintained and kept in
working condition. They keep the water system up and run-
ning, renovate buildings, install showers, paint, replace broken
roofs and do great "cement" work wherever it is needed.

Normally we refer to the spring and fall teams at the Hope
Center as 'work teams' but that designation is quickly becoming obsolete. Year by year these teams are becoming more ho-
listic in their focus and vision. Don't misunderstand! The teams
do plenty of hard work but as the Hope Center gradually becomes more and more polished, the teams are able to include a
variety of other ministries in their schedule as well.

Some of the same team members come back year after year.
Jack Dirnberger is in his 70's, has been to the Hope Center eight
times and is a specialist of the "underground" systems at the
Hope Center – the sewage systems! People like Barry Fluth,
Randy Porter and Rich Hendrickson are veterans at the Hope

Center. Year after year these wonderful workers have led the work teams that mostly come out of the same church in Minnesota.

To bolster our manpower, we occasionally invite past graduates of our International Vocational Academy to come back to camp to work for a fair daily rate. Team members and other supporters raise all the funds used to pay these graduates.

A variety of tasks were completed in 2009 that were very important to the Hope Center. We are now proud to welcome future teams to eat on our newly-poured dining room patio and climb the new steps to the intern building. We also completed new steps to the public restrooms near the entrance, finished the floor on the garage for our UTV, raised necessary sewer covers—bringing our entire system up to code—repaired and painted all the benches and installed a new electrical utility pole. We were also able to prep and begin the painting process on the exterior of two buildings and the interior of three more - all of which were completed by our staff before the camps began.

Many members of the work teams have been excited to be able to reconnect with IVA graduates from their previous trips, some from four and five years ago. As they worked side-by-side, old friendships strengthened and new ones were formed. The boys—as many as ten per day—worked hard and were receptive to the spiritual topics being presented by team members. Both Americans and Ukrainian youth participated in frequent prayer walks throughout camp asking for grace and blessing on all the people and ministries that come through our gates.

Some members choose to visit nearby villages with our program team to attend church, see the city center and go to the homes of new local friends. On a free evening many of the men even braved the traditional Russian *banya* (sauna).

Chapter 15

TEAMS - IMPRESSIONS
AND IMPACT

TO FOCUS ONLY ON THE MINISTRY AND THOSE BEING
ministered to would leave the "picture" we have tried to create
without an important element, the perspective of those who
partner with us at the Hope Center.

Randy Porter has been involved with the Hope Center from
the very beginning. Since his first trip in 2002, Randy has remained in shock at the progress that has been made since his
first visit - both at the facility and in the ministry programs. He
made it clear that he was pleased by the completion of the projects but that wasn't the only success. He felt that the team he
led in the spring of 2009 was unique - that all teams have their
own personality. He liked the balance of focus they achieved.
He recalled the early days when there was so much work to get
done that personal relationship seemed secondary to the tasks
completed. Now Randy is happy to see that communication,
cultural exchange and ministry opportunities are every bit as
valuable as the work projects.

David Forpahl has been on team trips three times. Last year
he brought a different perspective to his visit. David's single
purpose was to use the setting of workdays to minister to the
IVA graduates who came to work alongside the work team. He
felt the Lord was calling him to reconnect with three particular
young men whom he had befriended on previous trips.

Dave was only 72 hours into his trip before he had met all
three of them and even gained two more special friends. He
worked as hard as anyone but never resisted the Lord's lead-
ing to take his 'Three Amigos' on a prayer walk or spend some
time in the Word with them. He prayed for our programs, staff,
facilities and guests. One evening Dave felt compelled to write

the scripture passage Psalm 146 on strips of paper and gave them to all the graduates, encouraging them to read it that evening.

As Dave shared his heart for these young men he told us, "I can't possibly feel like I touched their lives as much as they touched mine."

We welcome work teams, summer teams, winter teams and interns year round. Come and be part of what the Lord is doing. We need everyone to come and make the Hope Center a beacon of light in an otherwise dark world.

Chapter 16

THE FUTURE

DURING THE COURSE OF THE YEAR MANY RESOURCES are sent out from the Hope Center. Our staff implements numerous programs. But, it is the people that these resources and programs touch that are the most important.

It is our prayer that what has been accomplished so far is only the beginning. We have tested programs and projects. Some worked well and should be continued. Others need refinement or, when necessary, to be discontinued. We are prepared to make those adjustments. We learn as we step forward in faith.

We believe that the Hope Center will continue to minister to orphans and disadvantaged children through the camps and through other programs year around. We pray that God will provide enough funding so we can resurrect the IVA program to its full potential. For that to work we need interns who are willing to give six months of their time to come serve with us.

One of our interpreters has been away for a year to get professional training so she can work with us in establishing a center to train future beauticians. This center will provide an invaluable resource and will help young ladies who are looking for training in this area and prepare them to find meaningful work.

We pray for more resources so we can use the Hope Center facilities and continue operating GLOMOS in Crimea. Our prayers go to a God we trust. We pray that He will use people who read this book to be instruments to fulfill His will for the Ukraine.

For years people in the West prayed for us behind the Iron Curtain. People prayed and gave resources to bring a few Bibles a year across the borders to us. Now the Curtain is down. You can freely bring Bibles and share the Gospel. Don't forget us now when there are such great possibilities. God's time for the Ukraine is now!

Chapter 17

WAYS TO GET INVOLVED

YOU ARE WELCOME TO JOIN THE TEAMS THAT TRAVEL to Ukraine each year. If you love children and have long arms, why not come and hug them and be part of the summer program teams. If you are good with a hammer and a paintbrush, please join one of the work teams. If you want to come and give two months or up to six months, please inquire about serving as an intern.

Visit *Global Action*'s website at www.globalaction.com for travel details and cost.

Without your prayers and gifts the Hope Center cannot move forward one single day. A stable flow of income makes it so much easier to reach out and minister daily to all these wonderful people who need so much.

Please feel free to give on the webat www.globalaction.com or call 1.888.725.3707 and give using your credit card. You may also write a check to *Global Action* and mail it to *Global Action* at: 7660 Goddard Street, Suite 200, Colorado Springs, CO 80920. Be sure to indicate on the memo portion of your check: "For: The Hope Center, Ukraine."

Further copies of this book can be ordered at www.globalaction.com

We ask that you please share this book with as many friends as possible.